MYSTERIES AND LEGENDS

of VIRGINIA

TRUE STORIES
OF THE UNSOLVED AND UNEXPLAINED

EMILEE HINES

gpp

Guilford, Connecticut

To Marian Barnard, Catherine Cantieri,
Dorothy Staffieri, Irene Stanley, and Elaine Trull,
who have all given me help and encouragement.

To buy books in quantity for corporate use
or incentives, call **(800) 962-0973**
or e-mail **premiums@GlobePequot.com.**

Project editor: Gregory Hyman
Text design: Lisa Reneson, Two Sisters Design
Layout artist: Kevin Mak
Map: M. A. Dubé © Morris Book Publishing, LLC

Library of Congress Cataloging-in-Publication Data is available on file.

ISBN 978-0-7627-5875-3

Printed in the United States of America

10 9 8 7 6 5 4 3 2 1

CONTENTS

Acknowledgments v

Introduction vii

Chapter 1   Grace Sherwood, the Witch of Pungo 1

Chapter 2   Virginia's Gentle Giant 14

Chapter 3   Lord Botetourt, the Mysterious Governor 29

Chapter 4   Was George Wythe Murdered? 43

Chapter 5   Seeking the Beale Treasure 56

Chapter 6   Who *Else* Killed Lucy? 69

Chapter 7   The Secret Seven Society 82

Chapter 8   The Curse of Hall's Store 87

Chapter 9   The Tunnel Vampire 102

Chapter 10   Was Anna Really Anastasia? 106

Chapter 11   The Murdered Mayor 120

Chapter 12   Sasha: Suicide or Murder? 133

Chapter 13   The Parkway Killer—or Killers 146

Chapter 14   Why the Shorts? 159

Bibliography 170

Index 179

About the Author 184

VIRGINIA

ACKNOWLEDGMENTS

A special thanks to Jerry Liedl, without whose help I could never manage to send a book to my editors.

I also want to thank Dennis Tennant at the *Daily Press* in Newport News; Randall Greenwell at the *Virginian Pilot*; Dale Neighbours at the Library of Virginia; Jamie Davis of the Virginia Historical Society; Rey Barry, who has an extensive Web site on Anastasia; Bill Rylance, Matt Riley, Bobby Page, Sidney Vaught, Johnny Barnard, Bill and Ruth Gibson, the reference staff at Henderson County Public Library; and my editors, Erin Turner and Meredith Rufino.

INTRODUCTION

Good stories are supposed to begin with Who, What, Where, When, Why, and How, because we want answers. One of the first and most persistent questions a child asks is "Why?" "Why is the sky blue?" or "Why do I look different from my friend?"

As we get older, we move on to questions such as "What happened?" "What caused it?" "What makes it work?" We take things apart to find out how they work, and we assemble the pieces of evidence to solve crimes or find the cure for a disease.

We are curious.

And we like stories. Legends are stories that have been told and retold as they pass down through generations, until it sometimes becomes difficult to separate fact from fiction. Virginia, being the oldest American colony and thus having the longest history, is the setting for many legends and mysteries.

Several legends concern Pocahontas, the Indian princess. Captain John Smith wrote that she laid her head over his on the execution block to save his life. Maybe she did, or maybe she asked her father—as his favorite daughter—to spare the captain's life. Or maybe Smith made the whole thing up. Whatever the truth is, it is legendary.

Other legends concern the origin of the Chincoteague ponies, the amazing feats of strength of Peter Francisco, the witchcraft of Grace Sherwood, and many other events that have often been told. Frequently, legends serve to inspire, such as those involving George Washington. He was said to have confessed to cutting down his father's cherry tree with a hatchet, saying, "I cannot tell a lie." He was then forgiven. His strength is illustrated by his throwing a silver dollar across the Potomac River.

Some of the mysteries in *Mysteries and Legends of Virginia* have never been solved and very likely never will be, as all the participants and witnesses are long dead. Some linger in our imagination; for example, wouldn't it be wonderful to find the Beale Treasure? At least two of the mysteries in this book were solved after the death of the mysterious person, and ironically, the same man was involved in both cases.

Other mysteries—a series of unsolved murders—may be solved by you, the reader. If you know or suspect details of an unsolved crime or know someone who may be a killer, be afraid, be very afraid. Then call the FBI.

CHAPTER 1

GRACE SHERWOOD, THE WITCH OF PUNGO

Witches in Virginia? Salem, Massachusetts, is known for hysterical accusations of witchcraft, witch trials, and twenty executions, but Virginia is not. Yet during the colonial period in Virginia, several women and one man were accused of performing black magic and witchcraft. The most famous case was that of Grace Sherwood, who was tried and convicted as the Witch of Pungo.

Witchcraft has been used to explain unusual and unfortunate happenings throughout the ages, and forms of witchcraft still exist, such as voodoo. Practitioners are usually envisioned as being robed and chanting around a fire deep in the woods, or cooking up trouble, like the three witches of Shakespeare's *Macbeth;* some people might think of the witch in Hansel and Gretel, who fattened children and then cooked and ate them. And there is Wicca, or good witchcraft, but witchcraft has traditionally been thought of as something evil and mysterious.

Recognizing the harm that witchcraft could do, the British Parliament passed a statute against it as early as 1607, during the reign of King James I of England. The penalty for dealing with the forces of evil ranged from a year in prison to a death sentence.

The first "test" to determine if someone was a witch was to have a group of citizens appointed by the sheriff search the accused for "marks of the devil." It was said that those who dealt with the devil and became his disciples had special teats or nipples on their bodies where the devil could suck. (Large moles or warts might be mistaken for these "devil's teats.") In addition, after such contact, the devil left dark marks that did not bleed "when pricked." Finding such marks was evidence that the accused should be tried for witchcraft in a court of law.

If the courts could not determine the guilt of an alleged witch, the accused was then put to the ultimate "test," being bound and dropped into deep water. Pure water was said to reject an evil person, so if the person floated, he or she was guilty of dealing with the devil and would thus be punished. If the accused sank, this proved innocence; but alas, it also caused the innocent's death.

In the Virginia Historical Society are records of fifteen witchcraft trials in colonial Virginia in the 1600s. No one was executed for the crime in Virginia, though in 1654 Katherine Grady was hanged on board a ship bound for Virginia when the passengers blamed her for causing a storm at sea.

Lower Norfolk County (later to become Princess Anne County and still later the City of Virginia Beach) was especially prone to belief in witchcraft. In 1655 several accusations of witchcraft circulated in Lower Norfolk County, causing general unrest. The justices of the county declared that if an accusation of witchcraft could not be proved, the accuser would have to pay a penalty of a thousand pounds of tobacco.

Despite the possibility of a heavy fine, the following year a clergyman brought a charge of witchcraft against William Harding. Harding was found guilty and was punished by ten lashes and banishment from the county, a different punishment from that required in King James's statute.

In 1676 a group of women were chosen to examine Jane Jenkins for marks of the devil, and in 1679 to search Alice Cartwright. In neither case were incriminating marks found, as far as the records show. Witchcraft was a popular belief, as evidenced by the publication in 1677 of John Webster's book *The Displaying of Supposed Witchcraft: Wherein is affirmed that there are many sorts of Deceivers and Imposters.* The stereotypical witch that we associate with Halloween devilry rides a broomstick, but in 1698 a neighbor accused Anne Byrd of riding her like a horse. There is no record of the outcome of this accusation of witchcraft. Was Byrd searched? Was her accuser punished?

Grace Sherwood was not anyone's idea of the stereotypical witch—an aged crone with bad teeth, wearing a black peaked hat and black robe, and cackling with laughter while committing

Grace was described as tall and well-built, a wife, midwife, and gardener.

Grace was born in 1660 to John White and his wife. The Whites owned land in Pungo, a fertile rural area lying just west of the Atlantic Ocean, bordered by bays and rivers. John White was also a carpenter, so the White family was well provided for. Grace must have been an only child, for after she married James Sherwood in 1680, her father willed all his property, including a 200-acre farm, to James, "my loving son-in-law." At the time of their marriage, James Sherwood already had a small farm, six head of cattle, two steers for plowing, and a comfortable cottage. Grace and James had three sons. Grace was thus a middle-class woman, busy with home and children, not at all the sort of impoverished woman who might make a Faustian deal with the devil in return for prosperity.

She was, however, outspoken and taller than many men, and in an era when women decorously wore dresses, Grace wore men's trousers when she worked outside.

Perhaps it was jealousy that led to accusations of witchcraft against her. Grace, who had a "green thumb," grew herbs and other plants to use as medicine and had a special way of healing. Plants thrived under her care, especially rosemary, which still flourishes near where she lived. A story spread that Grace bewitched a ship's cabin boy and caused swift winds to blow so that she could sail to England and back in a single night and bring rosemary sprigs to Pungo.

Another story was that when she was refused passage on a boat going to North Carolina, she vowed she would get there before the boat did. Sure enough, when the boat arrived, an eggshell was bobbing in the water, and Grace stepped out from it, assumed her normal size, and tied the eggshell to a tree limb with a bit of sewing thread.

In 1698 Grace was first formally accused of witchcraft by Richard Capps. Grace and James denied the charges and sued Capps for 50 pounds sterling. Capps didn't show up in court, and by some means he paid off the Sherwoods and made his peace, for there is no further court record of his claims.

Later the same year the Gisburne family's cotton plants began to wilt and die. At the same time, their pigs were behaving strangely, and some died. We might now think that the pigs had eaten some poison weeds or been poorly fed, and that a plant disease had infected the cotton. The Gisburnes had another answer: It was Grace Sherwood's fault. She was a witch and had put a curse on the family.

A short time later, Elizabeth Barnes claimed that Grace had entered her bedchamber, ridden her like a horse, and then disappeared through a keyhole or a crack beside the door, and that Grace sometimes changed herself into a black cat. Did Mrs. Barnes have a nightmare? Was she delusional? Again, the charge was that Grace Sherwood practiced witchcraft.

The Sherwoods' response to these absurd charges was a lawsuit for slander against the Gisburnes and the Barneses, asking 100 pounds sterling in damages from each couple. When the cases were heard, both defendant couples pled not guilty and were acquitted of slander by the jury. Not only did James and Grace have to bear the continuing stories against Grace, but they also had to pay the cost of bringing nine witnesses to court to testify in their behalf.

Perhaps stressed by the accusations and legal actions, James Sherwood died in 1701, and Grace was left to manage her farm with the help of her three sons. She was now a well-to-do widow with waterfront property, and the jealousy grew.

In 1705 Elizabeth Hill not only accused Grace of witchcraft but also beat her, causing "bruises and grievous injuries." Grace sued Mrs. Hill for assault, asking 50 pounds sterling in damages. We can imagine what a good lawyer would earn for his client now, but the county court awarded Grace only 20 shillings in damages.

Not content with this vindication, Luke and Elizabeth Hill filed suit to have Grace brought before the county court on charges of witchcraft. When the court met on January 3, 1706, Grace did not appear. Therefore the sheriff was ordered to "attach her body and answer the said summons next court"—in other words, Grace was subpoenaed. When court again convened on February 7, the Hills were ordered to pay court costs for the complaint, and the sheriff was ordered to summon a group of women to examine Grace for the telltale marks of witchcraft.

When the county court met on March 7, 1706, the jury of women reported as follows: "We the jury have searched Grace

Sherwood and have found two things like titts with several other spots." This jury was hardly impartial. Its forewoman was Elizabeth Barnes, the neighbor who had claimed that Grace had ridden her and slipped through a keyhole.

Nevertheless, based on this biased evidence, the justices of the county court decided that the matter must be taken up in General Court (made up of the governor and the Council). The Hills pursued the matter to the higher court, claiming that Grace had bewitched Mrs. Hill, and asked that the attorney general prosecute Grace Sherwood.

On April 16 the attorney general stated that he found the charge too general. Grace was not being charged with a specific act and therefore could not be prosecuted. He sent the case back to the county court. He suggested that they put Grace in jail until the matter was settled and that in the meantime they "make further enquiry into the matter."

The county court then issued a warrant for Grace's arrest and imprisonment until she could furnish security for her bond. Meanwhile, her body was to be examined once more, and her house was to be searched for objects of witchcraft, such as clay figures on which she had put a hex. There is no indication whether Grace's sons lived in the house to be searched, nor was there a specific list of objects to be seized.

When court next convened, on June 6, the prosecutor was Mr. Maximilian Boush, counsel representing Her Majesty, Queen Anne, in Virginia. A charge of witchcraft was taken seriously by the court. At this session it was stated that no objects pertaining to witchcraft had been found in the Sherwood home and that the group of women had refused to examine Grace. Were they afraid of Grace? Or did they consider the whole process ridiculous and not want to be part of it? They were therefore in contempt of court and should be dealt with "according to the utmost severity of the law." The court ordered that a new group of women be summoned to examine Grace Sherwood, who was again to remain in the sheriff's custody unless she could furnish security that would guarantee her appearance in court on July 5. It was further stated that Grace must exhibit good behavior toward Her Majesty the Queen and all her subjects.

It is unclear if Grace remained in jail or furnished the security, but it is likely that she remained in custody and that her three sons were now old enough to fend for themselves. The case was continued to the July 5 session of court.

At that session the small courthouse at New Town in Princess Anne County was crowded. Mr. Boush asked Grace to come forward to answer the charges. "You have heard yourself accused of being a witch. How do you plead?"

"I am innocent," Grace answered.

"Do you deny that you have had dealings with Satan?"

"I have had no such dealings. I have never met him."

"Do you deny that you have used your powers to bewitch others, to blight crops and animals?"

"I have no such powers," she said.

Grace's word was insufficient, and there was not enough evidence to convict her, but since the case had dragged on too long to be summarily dismissed, prosecutor Boush asked Grace if she would be willing to submit to the test by water.

Perhaps exhausted by trials and accusations and wanting to get the matter over with, she consented. If she had refused, it would have been taken as an automatic admission of guilt. But no matter how the water test turned out, she would lose.

The prosecutor then ordered the sheriff to take boats and men to assist him and to take Grace to Jonathon Harper's plantation at ten o'clock on the morning of July 9, to be dunked into deep water, "care always being taken to prevent her drowning."

On the first day appointed for the water trial, it was raining, and the court decided that riding to the plantation in the rain might be injurious to her health, as if the dunking would not be.

The following day, July 10, crowds from all over the county gathered well before the appointed hour to watch the test. A group of women searched Grace to make sure she was not carrying any objects of witchcraft or other objects that might place suspicion on her. After she was removed from the water, her body was to be searched again, to look for the telltale marks of devilry. We can imagine Grace's humiliation and frustration at being repeatedly stripped and searched.

The depth of the water at Harper's plantation was plumbed to make sure it was deeper than a man is tall, so that Grace could not stand on the bottom and save herself. She was cross bound: right finger to left foot, left finger to right foot. A thirteen-pound Bible was tied to her neck. Then the boat was rowed out from shore to the deepest water, and Grace Sherwood was thrown overboard with a great splash.

She may have thought of giving up at this point. Her husband was dead, her three sons had reached maturity, and she was worn out from the constant charges of witchcraft. If she allowed herself to sink, she would very likely drown but would be declared innocent of the charges. Her accusers would thus be proved wrong and would be fined for making false accusations. But her urge to live overcame her fatigue. After sinking only briefly, she bobbed to the surface, wrenched herself free from the bonds, and swam ashore.

The spectators gasped and began murmuring. So Grace Sherwood was indeed a witch. The appointed jury of "five elder, respectable women" examined her once more. Now that she had proved herself to be a witch, they felt more confident about reporting their findings. She was not like any other woman they knew of. She did indeed have two "things like titts on her private parts of a black color, blacker than the rest of her body."

The sheriff was therefore ordered to place Grace Sherwood in irons and take her to the jail for the colony—in Williamsburg—where she was to remain until further trial.

Reportedly, when Grace emerged from the water, she proclaimed, "I have been drenched, but so shall all of you be."

Then, although it was a cloudless day, a sudden clap of thunder, followed by a downpour, sent the spectators running for shelter.

Grace was not given the death penalty. Perhaps common sense prevailed and the justices realized the absurdity of deciding someone's guilt or innocence by whether or not the person could swim. She seems to have remained in jail for some years. Records of her imprisonment and any further trials may have been destroyed when the state courthouse was burned by invading Northern troops in 1865.

Records show that in 1708 Grace Sherwood paid a judgment of six hundred pounds of tobacco for some unknown levy and that in 1714 she paid back taxes on her property in Princess Anne County. She may have been quietly released by wise and sympathetic authorities, perhaps after her accusers—the Hills—had moved away or died.

In 1733 Grace made a will bequeathing her property to her three sons. The will was "proved" in 1740, indicating that Grace died in that year.

The manual for Virginia justices, published in 1736, described the crime of witchcraft but noted that there had been "very few instances" in Virginia. If the procedures laid out in this manual had been followed, Grace would not have been prosecuted. It specified that witches could be of either sex, who have been guilty of "conjuring, consulting or covenanting with evil spirits, entertaining, employing, feeding or rewarding

BILL RYLANCE

A sketch of what Grace Sherwood, convicted as a witch in 1704, might have looked like.

any such." Some specific prohibitions were taking up dead bodies or body parts to use as charms and using enchantment or charms to kill anyone or to cause any part of the body to be "wasted, lamed or destroyed." Also forbidden was using witchcraft to find treasure or lost objects, to provoke "unlawful Love," to destroy or harm anyone's cattle, or to attempt to destroy anyone's body, whether successful or not.

The manual states that prosecution should not take place without "strong and apparent cause, proved by sufficient witnesses, upon oath." This statute was in effect since 1607. Grace Sherwood had been accused, hauled into court, attacked, and put in danger of her life by illegal means, based only on gossip, hearsay, and the wild statements of jealous neighbors.

The dunking is remembered in two geographic names: The place where Grace Sherwood was dunked is called Witchduck Point, and a major street in Virginia Beach is named Witchduck Road. Books and articles have been written about Grace Sherwood, who was always called "The Witch of Pungo."

Beginning in the twentieth century, Virginia Beach has held an annual Pungo Strawberry Festival in the still-rural part of the city, and it includes a reenactment of Grace Sherwood's dunking. Local citizens take the part of the sheriff, the prosecutor, the witch, boatsmen, and an honorary mayor of Pungo. The honorary mayor's wife plays the part of the witch.

Those reenactments may now be at an end. On July 10, 2006, three hundred years to the day since Grace Sherwood's dunking, Virginia governor Tim Kaine issued a proclamation pardoning Grace posthumously. "With 300 years of hindsight, we all certainly can agree that trial by water is an injustice," Kaine wrote. "We also can celebrate the fact that a woman's equality is constitutionally protected today, and women have the freedom to pursue their hopes and dreams."

This pardon was brought about by the persistent efforts of Belinda Nash, of Old Ferry Farm. The courthouse where part of Grace's trial took place once stood on the farm's land. Nash's efforts brought national attention to Grace Sherwood and to Pungo, and she raised enough money to erect a statue of Grace, carrying a basket of rosemary and followed by a raccoon, a symbol of her love for animals. Even though Grace Sherwood's innocence has been established, a local church objected to her statue being placed near its property. The statue was finally set at Bayside Hospital, since Grace was a healer.

But she's not a witch anymore.

CHAPTER 2

VIRGINIA'S GENTLE GIANT

In 1765 Virginians were concerned about the growing taxation by the British king and Parliament, and some people resorted to smuggling to avoid taxation. Therefore little attention was paid when a dark-hulled ship made its way up the Appomattox River and anchored near the bustling docks of City Point—now Hopewell. A rowboat was lowered, and a little boy was set ashore. The rowboat returned to the ship, which sailed downriver and disappeared from view.

The boy, who appeared to be about five years old, did attract attention. Was someone supposed to meet him? Where were they?

The child didn't seem upset that the ship had left him, and he wandered about examining things. He had dark eyes, dark curly hair, and a swarthy complexion. He wore a tattered velvet suit trimmed in lace, and on his feet were shoes with silver buckles, one with the letter *P* and the other with the letter *F.*

As the day went on, the child began to cry. Various dock-workers tried to talk with him, to find out who he was, but he didn't speak English. He was given food and allowed to sleep in a warehouse, but authorities said that this was no suitable place for a child. If a home could not be found for him, he would be indentured to someone as a servant. In the meantime, he was taken to the Prince George County poorhouse.

Several days later Judge Anthony Winston stepped forward and offered to take the child to his home, Hunting Tower, in Buckingham County in central Virginia, west of Richmond.

Judge Winston pointed to himself and gave his name; then he pointed to the two letters on the boy's shoes.

"Pedro Francisco," the boy answered.

So he was probably Spanish or Italian, but since he had been abandoned and needed a home, he would become an American, a Virginian. And instead of Pedro, he would be called Peter. As Peter learned English, he told what he knew of his past: that he and his sister had been seized off the street near their home one Sunday morning. His sister was soon returned to the family, but Peter was taken on board a ship.

Judge Winston took Peter home with him, gave him a place to sleep, and assigned a slave to take care of him. The judge's wife apparently did not like Peter and did not allow him to be educated, perhaps because this would take time away from the work he could do around the plantation or perhaps because she resented the judge's attention to the strange boy. This lack of education was to change his future not once but twice.

As Peter became a teenager, he grew to over six feet tall and weighed more than 250 pounds. Judge Winston had Peter trained as a blacksmith, a trade in which his amazing size and strength would be an advantage. Peter was also intelligent and listened to political discussions around the dinner table. Judge Winston was Patrick Henry's uncle, and when Henry visited, the talk was always of independence.

In March 1775 Peter accompanied Judge Winston to Richmond, where delegates from all over Virginia gathered at St. John's Church to discuss what the colony should do about the British army and fleet taking over Boston and closing the port. The delegates agreed to form a militia, but Henry went further, describing the need to stand up to British power. He concluded with the famous, often-quoted words, "Give me liberty or give me death."

Peter was sixteen when the Declaration of Independence was signed the following year, and he begged to be allowed to join the Continental Army. At first Winston refused, but when Peter showed patience in not mentioning the matter for a month, the judge agreed. In October 1776 Peter became Private Francisco, a member of Company 9, called "The Prince Edward Musketeers," as most of the recruits came from Prince Edward, the county that adjoined Buckingham. Peter was now free of farm chores. He was issued a uniform and a musket and was promised one hundred acres of land at the end of the war and a monthly pay of $6.67 in the meantime. This would be the first money he had ever earned. He continued to grow both in height and weight and was a foot taller than the average recruit, who was five feet six inches.

Peter was always being tested, and there are numerous tales of his strength. He was said to be the strongest man in the Continental Army and probably the strongest man in America.

During early training, men were bragging about their skill with muskets, rifles, and bows and arrows, and one man boasted that he could hit any target with his tomahawk that others could hit with their muskets. Peter pointed to a spot on a pine tree, about ten feet up, and challenged the braggart to hit that spot. He did. Then Peter said, "Now how will you get your tomahawk?" The man realized he had been made to look foolish and started to attack Peter with a knife. Instead, Peter hoisted him up in the air with one hand, so the man could pull his tomahawk free.

On another occasion, a cow was stuck in a marshy area, lowing piteously. Peter waded into the muck, lifted the cow onto his shoulders, and carried her to safety.

In 1777 Company 9 joined another Virginia group to become Company 10 and marched north to Pennsylvania to become part of George Washington's army. In the battle of Brandywine, the Americans had more than 1,200 casualties, twice as many as the British. While others were retreating, Peter charged forward, and it was only after the battle that he realized he had been shot in the leg. He was taken to a nearby house to recover. Here the seventeen-year-old Peter met the nineteen-year-old Marquis de Lafayette, the French nobleman who had come to aid the American cause. General Lafayette, only three months in America, had also been wounded in the thigh. The two young men were quite different, in size, background (Lafayette was a nobleman, and Peter knew nothing of his parentage), experience, and rank (Lafayette was a general, and Peter was a private). Still, the two became friends and remained so until Peter's death fifty years later.

Peter's wound healed first, and he returned to duty. When the two men parted, Lafayette said that he wanted to give Peter a gift. At first Peter declined, but after a moment he said he would like a long sword. The ones issued to soldiers, he said, were too short for someone of his height. Lafayette promised that he would relay the message to General Washington, but the sword was a long time coming.

During the time that the Continental Army was encamped at Valley Forge, with all its horrors and privations, Peter was on special duty, spying on the British. Then he was sidelined by sickness for two months.

Later, because of his strength and fearlessness, he was made a member of the Light Infantry, a group much like the present-day Green Berets. In the battle of Monmouth, he was wounded in the thigh by a musket ball. The ball could not be removed and was to trouble him for the rest of his life. However, he was soon back in action, this time as one of General Anthony Wayne's special troops. Creeping silently through swamps under cover of darkness, the troops scaled the walls of the British fortress at Stoney Point. Peter was the second man over the wall. As Peter approached the sentry guarding the flagpole, the sentry slashed with his bayonet, opening a nine-inch wound in Peter's abdomen. Despite the injury, Peter thrust aside the sentry's bayonet and killed him.

When his enlistment was up in 1779, Peter—like many other recruits—left the army and returned to the Winstons' home, Hunting Tower, the only home he knew. He was welcomed as a hero and asked to tell of his time in the army. Many recruits signed up for only six weeks, a huge problem for General Washington in developing a strong army. Peter, however, had served three years and had been wounded three times, so he had much to tell.

After Peter had been at Hunting Tower a short while, a recruiter came through Buckingham County warning that Virginia needed militia for protection. The army of the British general Charles Cornwallis was winning battles in South Carolina, and if Virginians didn't join up and go there to protect that colony, Virginia might be invaded and conquered. Peter reenlisted.

On the morning of August 16, 1780, the Americans met Cornwallis's army on a narrow stretch of roadway near Camden, South Carolina. The untrained Virginia recruits were in front, with North Carolina militia behind them, and finally the seasoned Continental Army brought up the rear. Colonel William Mayo, commanding the Virginians, asked Peter to stay by his side, a wise move. Before the Americans were ready, the British charged, and the Virginia recruits turned and fled. Peter and Colonel Mayo continued to fight, and in the general retreat Peter saw the Americans' cannon mired in mud, the horses that were to transport it having been shot in their harness. The cannon could not be allowed to fall into British control. It was too important. Peter wrenched the 1,100-pound cannon free, an amazing feat of strength, and half-rolling, half-pushing it, he managed to get it safely behind American lines. This act was commemorated by a U.S. postage stamp issued on March 25, 1973.

Meanwhile, the British cavalry under Banastre Tarleton— called "the butcher" for his savagery in killing civilians as well as enemy soldiers—advanced. A cavalryman rode straight at Peter Francisco, who stepped aside at the last moment. The cavalryman wheeled and came at Peter again. Peter was ready and bayoneted the man, lifting him off the saddle. He captured the horse and rode to Colonel Mayo. Peter dismounted and offered the horse to his commander. Mayo accepted and rode to safety. In gratitude, he left Peter a thousand acres of land in his will.

Peter walked back to Buckingham County, thinking the war was over for him, but he was wrong.

Word reached Hunting Tower that Cornwallis was on the move, up through North Carolina. General Nathanael Greene was leading the American forces to counter the British general.

Peter joined a cavalry regiment formed in Prince Edward County and rode south toward Guilford Courthouse, near Greensboro, North Carolina. Soon after Peter's group joined the other American forces, wagons of supplies arrived from General George Washington. Included was a five-foot sword for Peter Francisco, promised by General Lafayette long ago at Brandywine. Peter was ready to fight.

The British troops were outnumbered more than two to one, but the Americans were mostly untrained and untried soldiers, whereas the British were battle-hardened professionals; moreover, the British were especially good with bayonets.

The battle began about noon on March 15. The North Carolina militia, in the front rank, killed many British troops, but when the remainder of the British forces kept coming, bayonets fixed and flashing in the late winter sunlight, many Carolina militiamen turned and ran. The Virginians, including Private Sam Houston, charged in from the sides. In the melee, Peter cut down eleven British troops with his sword but was wounded twice. The first injury came when a British soldier lunged at Peter, the tip of his bayonet going through Peter's calf and pinning him to his horse. If Peter moved, the wound would get worse. The soldier withdrew his bayonet, and Peter whirled and brought his sword down on the unfortunate man, splitting his head in two.

Although bleeding from his wound, Peter charged ahead of his fellow troops toward the British. This time the giant received a devastating injury. A British soldier bayoneted Peter, the point

LIBRARY OF VIRGINIA

*Portrait of Peter Francisco, the strongest man in the
American Revolution.*

of the bayonet entering at the knee and emerging where the
thigh joins the hip bone. Badly wounded, Peter managed to
crawl to the shelter of a tree.

As dusk came and rain began to fall, Cornwallis ordered
grapeshot fired into the mass of combatants, ending the day's
fighting. The Americans retreated, leaving the field to Cornwallis, who declared it a victory. However, he had lost nearly a third
of his troops, while the American had suffered much fewer losses.

General Greene, who was a Quaker, asked Quaker families
in the area to care for the wounded of both sides, and a Quaker

named Robinson came to Peter's aid. The family nursed him back to health over the next few weeks, and even found his famous sword and gave it back to him.

His horse long gone, Peter the cavalryman limped the two hundred miles home to Hunting Tower in Buckingham County. Only twenty-one years old, he had fought in several of the American colonies and had been injured six times. But he was still not through with the Revolutionary War.

Private Peter Francisco was offered a commission, but he declined. Officers had to write out documents and sign pay vouchers and requisitions for supplies, and Peter could not read or write.

Claiming victory, Cornwallis marched eastward. He urged British sympathizers to join his cause, but few did. Although he was slow to recognize it, his surrender was all but inevitable after the battle of Guilford Courthouse.

In recognition of the hero of that battle, General Greene sent Peter a set of seven razors specially inscribed, and in 1910 a monument was erected in honor of Peter Francisco. In addition, March 15 is honored as Peter Francisco Day.

Back home, Peter learned that the war had come to Virginia. Benedict Arnold had ravaged the Tidewater region and set fire to Richmond, and the dreaded Banastre Tarleton had come close to capturing Governor Thomas Jefferson. In his raid across Virginia, Tarleton stole any available horses and slit the throats of colts so that Virginians would not have any horses.

Even at home, as a civilian, Peter still performed feats of bravery. Once, he was at a tavern near Burkeville when he heard troops approaching. He ran outside, only to be stopped by an armed man. Eight others approached and went into the tavern, leaving Peter to be guarded by a single man. The guard demanded money, but Peter had none. Then he asked for Peter's silver knee buckles. When the guard bent to take them off Peter, Peter grabbed the man's sword and killed him with it. Other soldiers ran out, and Peter wounded several, calling out to his imaginary companions. The soldiers saw Tarleton's legion riding toward them and cried out "Ambush." The legion turned back, and the troops fled from the tavern. Peter gathered their horses and led them home to Buckingham. He sold all but one, which he kept and named Tarleton.

Peter rode his horse Tarleton to join Lafayette and Washington at Yorktown and witnessed the surrender of General Cornwallis. Although there would be other battles for another two years, Cornwallis's surrender essentially marked the end of the Revolutionary War.

Legend says that Peter was walking with Lafayette past St. John's Church in Richmond when a lovely young lady tripped and fell right into Peter's arms. She thanked him for catching her and went her way. Peter was smitten, but he didn't know the young lady's name.

Two days later, one of Lafayette's aides, Major Richard Anderson, invited the two to join him at a gathering at the

Cumberland County home of the Carringtons. It was on the way to Buckingham, so Peter was glad to accept. To his surprise, one of the guests was Major Anderson's daughter Susannah, the very young lady he had fallen in love with. However, both the Anderson and Carrington families expected her to marry George Carrington. Peter professed his love and asked her to marry him. She too was smitten with the dark haired, dark-eyed giant. She accepted his proposal but said that he had to ask her father's permission.

Peter approached Major Anderson, who told Peter that he was unacceptable: He was uneducated and had no home and no way to support a wife. Peter agreed that these charges were true, and he set out to remedy them. He learned to read and write and read every book he could lay his hands on. He set himself up as a blacksmith and storekeeper in Buckingham and applied for the land and bounty he had been promised for his military service.

In 1782 Susannah's father died. She inherited sixty acres of land, and her brothers had no objection to the marriage, so she and Peter Francisco were married in December 1784. For five years the couple was happy and prosperous. They had three children, one of whom died soon after birth. Then Susannah died, and Peter was left with two small children to care for.

Peter took the children on regular visits to Susannah's family, and there he met one of her friends, Catherine Brooke, from a socially prominent Tidewater family. The two were married in 1794 and had twenty-seven years together. They had two sons and two daughters. Peter continued to operate the store and ordinary—or inn—and accumulated several tracts of land.

Periodically, men would arrive to challenge the giant. One was so persistent that Peter picked him up and set him over the fence. "What about my horse?" the man demanded. Obligingly, Peter lifted the horse and set it over the fence beside its owner.

Another story told about Peter Francisco was that he had a dozen large chairs specially built and gave them to the friends he visited most often, so that he could use these and not break his friends' chairs.

After Catherine's death in 1821, Peter met the English-born widow Mary Grymes West. She was forty, he sixty-one. They were married in 1823, but this marriage was not as successful as Peter's earlier two had been. The third Mrs. Francisco didn't like the rustic life Peter led, and when an invitation came for Peter to visit with Lafayette on his travels in America in 1824, she refused to accompany her husband. She felt that she would be embarrassed by her clothes and their carriage. So Peter went without her.

He rode to Yorktown, where Washington's victory in 1781 was celebrated, and then accompanied Lafayette to Williamsburg, to Norfolk, and then by steamer to Richmond, where the festivities went on for days. He went with Lafayette as far as Petersburg and then returned to Buckingham.

To please his wife, Peter gave up his dream of being a plantation owner and his happy days riding about the countryside.

Instead, he accepted a job as sergeant-at-arms of the Virginia legislature, which paid a small stipend. In addition, he had his Revolutionary War pension at last, and he was given an apartment for nominal rent. His wife was still not satisfied and spent much of her time with her daughter in Fincastle.

For six years Peter went faithfully to the legislature, until one morning in January 1831 when he sent word that he was ill. One of Peter's children, who lived in Petersburg, asked Episcopal Bishop Channing Moore to check on his father. The bishop was appalled at Peter's condition. The Virginia giant, now seventy-one, had been ill for nearly three weeks and could get no relief from his pain. He may have had a burst appendix. He died on January 16, and after a huge funeral with many eulogies, he was buried in Richmond's Shockoe Cemetery.

The mystery of Peter's birth was not solved for more than another century. Dr. John Manahan, a genealogist who was later to achieve fame as the husband of Anna Anderson, the supposed Anastasia, had a grant for study in Portugal. He had long heard rumors that Peter Francisco might have been Portuguese. He searched out records of families named Francisco, and on the island of Terceira in the Azores, he found what he was looking for. There was the record of a boy named Pedro born on July 9, 1760, which would have made him five when he was put ashore in Virginia in 1765. The same record listed other children in the family, along with the dates of their birth, marriage, and death. For Pedro there was only the birth date.

The descendants of Peter Francisco meet annually to celebrate their ancestor, and various Portuguese American groups count him as one of their own. Monuments have been built in his honor, and he has been called "the most extraordinary soldier of the Revolution" and "the American Hercules." America owes a huge debt of gratitude to this Virginia giant. But the mystery of why he was kidnapped will probably never be solved.

CHAPTER 3

LORD BOTETOURT, THE MYSTERIOUS GOVERNOR

Norborne Berkeley, the fourth Baron Botetourt and royal governor of Virginia, was the subject of mysteries both in life and in death. According to one source, when the governor arrived in Virginia in 1768, he was bankrupt. Yet when an inventory of his belongings was made after his death two years later, the list ran to nineteen pages and included more than 16,500 items, many of them luxury goods. How did he acquire all this? Were his purchases of items to bring to Virginia the cause of his bankruptcy? Moreover, soon after his arrival he made generous donations to Bruton Parish Church and Princeton University and for the establishment of an almshouse for the poor in Williamsburg, and he was almost single-handedly responsible for the building and maintenance of the first institution for the insane in America.

Critics asked why he chose to come to Virginia at all. For sixty years, royal governors had remained in England, collecting their salaries and sending substitutes to serve in the colonies. Yet Botetourt came to Virginia at a time of deep conflict between the colonies and King George III. The king and Parliament expected the American colonies to pay the costs of the French and Indian War and therefore imposed a series of taxes. The colonists protested and boycotted imported products, and eventually most of the taxes were rescinded. Why would a royal governor, a baronet, choose this time to come to an outpost of the empire, away from the power center of London?

Rumors alleged that the baron had suffered huge gambling losses, but there is no evidence of his gambling as governor of Virginia. He did have a dozen decks of playing cards among his belongings in the palace, but none of his guests ever mentioned winning money from the governor or losing to him. One source says that Botetourt was in debt because of his generosity to the needy and to his kin and that he had made a bad investment in a copper works.

What had Lord Botetourt done to earn his peerage? The title had been "in abeyance"—not used by anyone—for more than three hundred years, since the last holder died in 1406. In 1764 Norborne Berkeley, then serving as a member of Parliament for Gloucestershire, was made one of the Lords of His Majesty's Bed Chamber and given the title Baron Botetourt. From then until his departure for Virginia, he served in the House of Lords. He had earlier received the honorary title Lord Lieutenant of Gloucestershire.

The baron had an illegitimate son, Charles Thompson, born about 1740, when Norborne Berkeley was twenty-two. In most cases of illegitimacy, the mother is known, and if there is a mystery, it is the identity of the father. In this case, it is the mother's identity that is unknown. She must have been named Thompson, and she must have been of the upper classes, as Charles Thompson became a vice admiral in the Royal Navy and had the baronetcy of Virkees created for him. Thompson married well, to the Lady Jane Selby; fathered five children; and named a son Norborne, who succeeded him as baronet. Why did Berkeley choose not to marry the mother of his only child?

Whatever his reasons for accepting the post in Virginia, Lord Botetourt was warmly welcomed. An example of his acceptance was a letter from Colonel George Mercer in London, writing to his brother in Virginia: "I congratulate you and my country on the appointment of Lord Botetourt to the government of Virginia."

The British government, aware of the rebellious feelings stirring among Virginians, may have chosen Botetourt because he was titled and because he had a commanding, attractive presence. To make sure that Botetourt made a good first impression, the king had had the new governor conveyed to his post in Virginia in a seventy-four-gun ship of the Royal Navy. On board the ship with Botetourt were a splendid coach and a team of matched gray Hanoverian horses, a gift from the Duke of Cumberland, the king's uncle. Adding to the appearance of opulence, the horses' harnesses were silver. On October 26, 1768, his ship landed at "Little England" plantation on the Hampton

River, where the governor was greeted with lavish ceremonies and a cannon salute. Traveling overland in the coach, dressed in a scarlet suit with gold braid, he beheld his capital city, Williamsburg. He did not appear to be bankrupt. The members of the governing council escorted him to the capitol, where he took the oath of office. The group then went to Raleigh Tavern for a celebratory banquet. It was a propitious beginning.

In his first speech to the House of Burgesses, Botetourt declared himself a "sincere friend" of Virginia, who would take every care for the colony's welfare. At the same time, he added that he was "a faithful servant of the best of sovereigns," King George III. Botetourt thus had to serve two interests in order to bridge the gap between king and subjects.

He was soon confronted with a challenge to royal authority. Members of the House of Burgesses, considering what had been happening in Massachusetts, where the British closed the port of Boston to punish the colony for its rebellious outbreaks, chose to express their objections to acts of Parliament that they felt infringed on all colonists' rights. They drew up a petition stating that they opposed taxation without representation and the practice of taking defendants accused of sedition to England for trial, away from possible witnesses. When the burgesses presented the petition to the governor to be sent on to the king, Botetourt told them, "I have heard all your resolves, and augur [predict] ill of their effect. You have made it my duty to dissolve you; and you are dissolved accordingly." They were locked out of the capitol building.

Undaunted, they went to nearby Raleigh Tavern and signed the Virginia Non-importation Resolutions on May 18, 1769, agreeing to boycott imported goods until the Revenue Act was repealed and Americans accused of sedition were tried in their own colonies. British merchants pressured Parliament to rescind the hated measures. In November 1769 Lord Botetourt called a special session of the burgesses to pass on to them a letter from Lord Hillsborough, the colonial secretary, saying that taxes had been withdrawn on all items except tea. The price of tea in the colonies, moreover, was priced cheaper than in London.

So the matter was smoothed over, and Governor Botetourt became involved in the unsuccessful effort to grow grapes for wine in Virginia. A certain amount of tea was smuggled, and local substitutes such as sassafras were always available. Elsewhere, reaction to the tea tax was violent, but Virginians liked their governor.

Botetourt was fond of his residence, the Governor's Palace, and its extensive gardens. He delighted in walking among the holly gardens and boxwood mazes to the canal. The garden was walled, giving him privacy.

But he was not a solitary man. He entertained lavishly, noting at one point that fifty-two people had dined with him that day and that he expected that many or more on the following day. By December 1769 it seemed that the burgesses had forgiven the governor, for they gave him an elaborate ball.

The following autumn, less than two years after his triumphal arrival, the governor suddenly fell ill and died on October 14, 1770. His death was explained as "a fever," and some burgesses thought that perhaps the stress of the political situation had caused his illness. Could it have been food poisoning? Typhoid? Until the time of his sudden illness, the governor had appeared hale and hearty.

Most Virginians grieved over Botetourt's death, but not Thomas Jefferson, who thought that Botetourt's death was good luck for the Revolution. Later, assessing the Revolution, he wrote, "Lord Botetourt's great respectability, his character for integrity, and his general popularity, would have enabled him to embarrass the measures of the patriots exceedingly. His death was, therefore, a fortunate event for the cause of the Revolution."

Botetourt's funeral was the most elaborate and expensive in Virginia up to that time, costing 700 pounds. Hundreds attended the service in Bruton Parish Church and followed the silver-trimmed coffin to Wren Chapel at the College of William and Mary. Governor Botetourt had expressed a wish to be buried in Virginia, and as he was on the Board of Visitors of the college, the crypt under the floor of the chapel seemed an appropriate burial site.

Even before the funeral, the General Court had met to choose executors for the governor's estate. These had to be the most prominent, trustworthy men of the colony, as befitted the rank and importance of Baron Botetourt. Heading up the committee was William Nelson, president of His Majesty's Council and acting governor until a new royal governor could be chosen by the king. Assisting him were John Randolph, the attorney general, and Robert Carter Nicholas, treasurer of the colony. They hired the governor's secretary, Peter Pelham, and his servant and chief household officer, William Marshman. The two men were to assist

Medallion honoring Norborne Berkeley, Lord Botetourt, Governor of Virginia, who died suddenly after only two years in office.

the executors for the length of the inventory of the late governor's effects, or up to one year. The task of drawing up the inventory of the contents of the sixty-one-room Governor's Palace was formidable, but Nicholas, Pelham, and Marshman did such a thorough job that the list was used as a guide when the Colonial Williamsburg Foundation in the twentieth century attempted to restore and furnish the palace. Visitors today see the Governor's Palace as it must have looked when Governor Botetourt was in residence.

Baron Botetourt's heir was not his illegitimate son, but his nephew, Henry Somerset, fifth Duke of Beaufort, and it was he who decided the disposition of Botetourt's property: what should be sent to England, what should stay in Virginia. The title Baron de Botetourt was once more abeyant, but it was revived in 1803 so that Beaufort also became the fifth Baron Botetourt.

We can learn a great deal about someone by studying his personal effects: What kind of clothing did he have? What did he eat and drink? What books did he read? What food and clothing did he provide for his slaves? Lord Botetourt's personal property was especially revealing, but it also brings up questions about the man and his life.

The inventory listed which furniture belonged to the colony of Virginia, most of it "looking glasses" (of which there was one in nearly every room), framed prints and paintings, and chairs, as well as two walnut tables with sixteen accompanying chairs and a sideboard with a marble top. For the most part, however, Lord Botetourt himself furnished the Governor's Palace in fine fashion. Indeed, it would have taken most of the cargo area of his ship to bring it all to Virginia, and the contents of pantries and closets are mind-boggling.

Among the most intriguing items are two that treasurer Nicholas held for safekeeping: a lady's picture in miniature and a diamond ring listed "for Lady Winne." Who was the "lady" in the picture? Was it Lady Winne? Who was she, and why did the governor have a diamond ring for her? Was she perhaps the unidentified mother of his son? Was he intending marriage, or was it just a generous gift to some Virginian or English beauty?

How did Nicholas know that the diamond ring was intended for Lady Winne? Did the governor leave a note stating this? What became of the ring? Neither of these items was on the list of property that the Duke of Beaufort requested to be sent to England.

We know that Lord Botetourt, like many readers before and since, borrowed books and failed to return them. The inventory noted: "Books doubtful to whom they belong." This included three books of journals sent to George Wythe; one book on the flora of Virginia, said to belong to a Mr. Clayton; the third volume of *Rapin's History;* and three volumes of Sherlock's sermons, the latter thought to have been in the mansion when Botetourt arrived. And he also must have loaned books, as several sets were noted as having a volume missing.

He had an eclectic collection of books, nearly three hundred volumes, which was a large library for that time. He had one Bible and one prayer book, but eleven dictionaries. At least one of these was in French. Others included a law dictionary, a gardener's dictionary, and a marine dictionary. As would be expected, the governor owned sets of Virginia laws and journals of the House of Burgesses as well as the acts of the previous British monarch, George II, and numerous histories. His library also included Greek writings, several books in French, the contemporary novels *Tom Jones* and *The Adventures of Joseph Andrews* (one volume missing), and Jonathan Swift's satires. In addition, he had several books on military behavior, though there is no record that he ever served in the military.

The governor's furniture was mostly mahogany: tables, writing desks, bedsteads, dressers, even fire screens and wine coolers. To warm the spacious rooms, he had imported several "Dutch stoves" that burned coal, for downstairs. These were still on order when he died. All rooms also had wood-burning fireplaces, which were cleaned, lighted, and replenished by servants.

Many of the items are things we no longer use: bootjacks for removing tight-fitting boots, wig stands and powder for wigs, toasting forks, bed-warming pans, chamber pots, flat irons, and sugar hatchets to chop up loaves of sugar. Several birdcages are listed, but there is no mention of the birds. Did Botetourt have a parrot? Canaries?

He did have three sets of surveyor's instruments and a case of surgical instruments, though he was obviously not a surgeon. Also listed were a pair of pistols "in furniture," meaning their wooden case; five swords; a bow and arrows; and a "fowling piece," or hunting rifle. Botetourt was well equipped for self-defense.

As might be expected for someone who had to entertain regularly, the governor owned many sets of silver utensils, hundreds of plates, cups, saucers, beer glasses, wineglasses, and water glasses. Even his servants had ample sets of Staffordshire china, which his heir specified was not to be sent to England.

The food and drink listed in the inventory are especially interesting. Botetourt was drinking and serving tea, though it was taxed, as well as two kinds of coffee, and in his storeroom were twenty-four pounds of chocolate. He was fond of "sweet meats," or candied fruit, and in his storeroom were three kinds of sugar (fifty-nine loaves in all), from single refined to treble refined. His smokehouse held 133 "pieces of bacon," which at that time could mean any kind of smoked pork.

The immense quantities of alcohol might lead us to suspect liver damage. On the main level of the mansion, convenient for serving, were forty bottles of rum, as well as cider, burgundy, and Madeira. There was a special beer cellar, and in the wine cellar and vault were more than a thousand bottles of wine and brandy.

In the coach house were the grand state coach and the six gray horses that had brought the governor to Williamsburg, and in other buildings were harnesses and saddles, livestock feed, gardening implements, and other livestock. The governor's establishment was like a small village, complete unto itself. One small mystery is in the poultry listing, which included turkeys, geese, and ducks, but no chickens. Why not? Where did the governor's cook get eggs?

Botetourt was well dressed, without doubt. Besides the various suits and coats, he had eighty-five pairs of stockings, fifty-six ruffled shirts, and thirty-two pairs of shoes. And he was still ordering more at the time of his death. Several items arrived after the inventory began.

The Duke of Beaufort requested all the books and maps, the various shoe buckles, surveyor's instruments, snuffboxes, silverware, china, linens, pistol, swords, and "three pipes of Madeira to be filled and well casked."

The ceremonial coach, the king's portrait, and the "warming stoves" were given to the House of Burgesses. Botetourt's estate included only 57 pounds sterling in cash, hardly enough to pay for shipping to England the items his nephew wanted. The executors sold the remaining items and the governor's six slaves, paid off the pledges the governor had made to Virginia charities, and sent the remaining money to the duke. The goods the duke requested were packed, and space on a ship was finally found. In March 1772 the Duke of Beaufort wrote that the ship and cargo were probably lost.

Less than a year after Botetourt's death, in July 1771, the burgesses voted funds for a marble statue of the governor to be placed in the capitol at Williamsburg. Richard Hayward, whose sculptures had been placed in Westminster Abbey, was chosen to carve Botetourt's likeness. A medallion showing the late governor in profile was sent to Hayward, who reported that he had found a fine block of marble. In May 1773 the finished statue arrived by ship in Virginia, accompanied by one of Hayward's assistants.

The statue was set up in the piazza between the two wings of the capitol, with plaques bearing inscriptions to the late governor. So popular had Botetourt been that his statue was not harmed during the Revolution, though those of other British authorities were vandalized, and it was regularly cleaned by order of the burgesses until 1779, when the capital was moved to Richmond. Governor Botetourt's statue, along with the colonial capitol and the rest of Williamsburg, sank into neglect. Eventually the head and a hand of the statue were knocked off and damaged.

In 1801 the College of William and Mary bought the statue from the State of Virginia, restored it, and moved it onto the college grounds. Incoming freshmen were expected to curtsy or to doff their hats to the statue, and it became a focal point and meeting place on campus. After years of weathering, however, the statue was moved into Swem Library, and a replica now stands before the Wren Building.

Meanwhile, what happened to Botetourt's body?

A fire in 1859 burned the Wren Building and its adjoining chapel, leaving only a brick shell. While work was beginning on reconstruction, Hugh Grigsby, a wealthy patron of the college, decided to explore the crypt. Plaques on the wall were too charred to be legible, but it was generally believed that Governor Botetourt and Sir John and Lady Randolph had been buried there nearly a century before. Removing planks in the floor of the chapel, Grigsby entered the crypt. One large vault held two sets of bones, one of them in a coffin with six circular handles, which Randolph's was said to have had. The body next to him therefore must have been that of Lady Randolph. At some distance was the coffin of Peyton Randolph, well labeled.

Was the largest coffin that of Baron Botetourt? The coffin itself was iron. Its lid, of wood covered by black cloth, had rotted, and its contents were eerie. There were long thigh bones, vertebrae, and arm bones, but no ribs or skull. What had happened to the remains of the beloved governor? He definitely had not "rested in peace."

A silver plaque identifying Botetourt's remains was placed on the coffin, and the crypt was resealed. In 1862, when Union forces invaded Williamsburg, they broke into the crypt and stole the plaque. Thirty years later it was returned to the college by a New York jeweler to whom it had been sold. Around the turn of the twentieth century, the crypt was opened to make certain the governor's remains were there. They were, but in 1969 looters broke into the crypt looking for valuables and scattered all the bones.

Where is the governor's skull? Some fraternity members have claimed to have seen the skull and to have used it for a drinking cup in initiations, but no one has brought forth the skull as proof. So who can say? Governor Botetourt, a convivial man, might have liked that outcome for his remains.

CHAPTER 4

WAS GEORGE WYTHE MURDERED?

When George Wythe was eighty, an age much older than most of his compatriots reached, the esteemed law professor, patriot, and signer of the Declaration of Independence sat up in bed, seriously ill, and announced, "I am murdered!"

But was he? Or was his suspicion all wrong? One of his servants had died hours after Wythe fell ill, and another had been gravely ill at the same time but was recovering. Could they have succumbed to typhoid, cholera, or some other common illness, or had all three been poisoned?

The young man accused of Wythe's murder was acquitted, for reasons that today would not happen.

George Wythe's life was deeply affected by the deaths of those he loved. When he was only three, his father died, leaving his mother, Margaret Wythe, with three children to care for. Under the laws of entail, George's older brother, Thomas, would inherit the family plantation, Chesterville, near present-day Langley, Virginia, when he reached the age of eighteen. George and his sister would receive a few items, and their mother could remain on the plantation for the rest of her life.

Margaret realized that her second son would have to earn a living some way other than being a planter, so she set out to educate him. She was the daughter of well-educated Quakers and gave her son a strong classical education in Latin and Greek, including the laws of those civilizations.

When George was sixteen, he was sent to live with his mother's sister Elizabeth and her husband, Stephen Dewey, in Charles City County. Dewey was a lawyer, and George became his apprentice and assistant, "reading law." Because there were no law schools in Virginia at the time, reading law under the instruction of a practicing attorney was the way to become a lawyer. (This practice was permitted until the early twentieth century.) Applicants did have to pass the bar exam.

Virginians were not as litigious then as they are now, for there were no corporations or "deep pockets" to sue, but George experienced a wide variety of cases. Besides the usual murder and assault cases, there were cases involving theft, destruction of property, libel, boundary disputes, and stolen elections. Wills had to be drawn up, estates settled, dowries negotiated, real estate bought and sold. Years later, his death would be the cause of one of Virginia's most famous trials.

To pass the bar, young lawyers had to be questioned by a panel of lawyers, pay a 20 shilling fee, and present a certificate of good character. George was admitted to the bar in 1746, soon after his mother's death. Not wishing to live with his brother and be always in his shadow, George moved to Spotsylvania County to work as an assistant to Zachary Lewis. He fell in love with his employer's daughter Ann, and the two were married in December 1747. Less than a year later, Ann died.

George Wythe then moved to Williamsburg, Virginia's capital. He applied to be a clerk to the House of Burgesses, the governing body of the colony, and was accepted. Because the burgesses met for only a short time each year, he had ample time to develop a law practice. Wythe was scrupulously honest, sometimes returning a client's money if he felt he had been overpaid, and Wythe occasionally declined to represent someone he thought guilty or "in the wrong." In 1754 he was elected to represent Williamsburg in the House of Burgesses.

The following year, another death changed the course of George's life: his brother Thomas died unexpectedly, and George inherited Chesterville. He was also appointed justice of the Elizabeth City County Court, a position his brother had held. George was a man of property, but he didn't want to leave Williamsburg, for he had fallen in love with Elizabeth Taliaferro. The two were married in 1755, when George was twenty-nine and Elizabeth sixteen. As a wedding gift, her father built them a handsome brick home close to the Governor's Palace in Williamsburg.

Wythe became a close friend of Governor Francis Fauquier, a cultured gentleman interested in the arts and science and a member of the Royal Society. The governor and Wythe often

George Wythe, jurist and law professor, as he looked shortly before his death.

dined together, and the governor arranged musical performances that included the talented student and violinist Thomas Jefferson, who became Wythe's most famous law student.

Wythe hired Hamilton St. George to manage Chesterville, giving him generous terms: all the fuel and "provisions for his table" that St. George required, including slaughtering Wythe's livestock. Wythe later bitterly regretted this. When the royal governor Lord Dunmore fled from Williamsburg to the Norfolk area in 1775 and began attacking Virginia plantations and cities, St. George fed Dunmore's troops with Chesterville goods.

As trouble grew between England and the colonies, delegates from the colonies met in Philadelphia for the Continental Congress. Wythe was one of Virginia's delegates, and he and Elizabeth made the journey in a rapid six days and then were stricken with smallpox, so that it was autumn before Wythe began to speak before the Congress.

The Wythes remained in Philadelphia for 241 days, until the Declaration of Independence had been drafted. They returned to Williamsburg, where George was too late to help write the Virginia constitution, but he did design the Great Seal of Virginia, relying on his classical studies for inspiration. George and Elizabeth returned to Philadelphia in the autumn of 1776, when he signed the Declaration of Independence, though all the signers knew that doing so was committing treason against the king.

Wythe and Jefferson spent the next two years revising the laws of Virginia, and Wythe was then named a professor at William and Mary College. He was proud of the little college, which had up-to-date scientific equipment and a library of three thousand volumes. The capital was moved to Richmond in 1780, and the Williamsburg capitol building and Governor's Palace were abandoned. During the final battles of the Revolutionary War, Wythe offered his house to George Washington. French troops were quartered in the college and American troops in the former Governor's Palace. In the next few months, both burned. With financial help from the king of France and the king of England, the college was rebuilt, and Wythe went back to teaching. His knowledge of the law was legendary, and students vied to attend his lectures.

In 1787 Wythe was again called to serve his country by helping to draft a constitution for the new nation. He went to Philadelphia and began work, but he had to return quickly to

Virginia because of his wife's illness. Elizabeth died on August 18, only forty-eight years old.

Wythe went on teaching at the college for three more years. In addition, he taught private students in his home, was a leader in Virginia's ratification of the U.S. Constitution, and was named chancellor (judge) of the Virginia Court of Chancery, which was concerned mainly with property rights. In this position he ruled that independence from Britain did not wipe out the debts that Americans owed to British merchants. His decision, though unpopular, was upheld by the U.S. Supreme Court.

In 1791 Wythe moved to Richmond to be close to his job, taking a house on Shockoe Hill. He had long ago freed his slaves, but two of his former slaves went along to Richmond as paid servants: Lydia Broadnax, his cook and housekeeper; and Michael Brown, a teenage mulatto whom Wythe was educating. In his will Wythe provided that a large portion of his estate would go to Michael Brown, and his education was to be under the supervision of Thomas Jefferson. The remainder of the estate would go to Wythe's sister's grandson, George Wythe Sweeney. Sweeney's father, who was also named for the judge, had been helpful in managing Chesterville, the Wythe plantation.

Wythe invited the eighteen-year-old Sweeney to live with him in Richmond, thinking he might be a good influence on the wild youth. Instead, Sweeney ran up huge gambling debts. He stole several valuable books, silver cups, and other items from his great-uncle and sold them. Next he forged four checks, signing

the judge's name to them. Each time the bank called the forger-
ies to the judge's attention. Wythe said that he would speak to
the young man and that it would not happen again.

Lydia Broadnax caught Sweeney in the act of reading
Wythe's will while the judge was at court. Sweeney would have
discovered that he was not the sole heir: Michael Brown was an
equal inheritor, but if Michael died before Wythe, then Sweeney
would get the entire estate.

On Sunday morning, May 25, 1806, Wythe went through
his usual routine. He had rigged up a shower in the backyard
and doused himself with cold water, dressed, and went up to his
room. He rang a bell to signal to Lydia Broadnax that he was
ready for breakfast.

She had made the usual big pot of coffee, and the food was
almost ready when Sweeney burst into the kitchen, demanding
a piece of toast and a cup of coffee immediately. She told him
that breakfast would be ready in a few minutes and that he could
eat with the judge. He refused to wait, poured himself a cup of
coffee, and waved his hand over the pot. Then he went to the
fireplace and threw a paper in it to burn. He left soon after.

Lydia took Wythe his breakfast, and back in the kitchen
she and Michael Brown ate breakfast and drank coffee. While
Michael had a second cup of coffee, she emptied the grounds and
washed the coffee pot.

Wythe ate his eggs and toast and sipped coffee while he read
the newspaper. Suddenly he was hit with stomach cramps and

searing pain throughout his body. He managed to pull himself up from his chair before he vomited on the floor. Staggering down the stairs, he asked Lydia to send for a doctor. Lydia was doubled over with cramps and clutching her abdomen, and Michael was slumped over the table, convulsing. He would die within a week.

Not one but three eminent doctors came to treat Wythe. Dr. James McClurg, who had been a colleague of Wythe's as professor of anatomy at William and Mary College, had also been a delegate with Wythe to the Constitutional Convention. His nephew, Dr. James McCaw, had inoculated thousands of Virginians in 1794, thus avoiding an epidemic of smallpox. Dr. William Foushee, Wythe's personal physician, had been the mayor of Richmond. All three doctors had studied medicine in Edinburgh, Scotland.

Although Wythe told the doctors that he and his servants had been poisoned, the doctors declared that the three had cholera. Indeed, some of the symptoms were the same: Both cholera and arsenic poisoning cause diarrhea, vomiting, and stomach cramps. However, in cholera the victim's skin becomes silvery blue, the fingernails turn blue at the base, and the victim dies within a few hours. All three in the Wythe household remained alive for at least a week; cholera is almost always spread by contaminated water, not private wells such as Wythe had; and no cases of cholera had ever been reported in the Richmond area.

The doctors refused Wythe's request to search his great-nephew's room for evidence of arsenic. Even if it were found, it would prove nothing, they said, for the most common kind of arsenic, ratsbane, had been used for centuries to kill rats and was an ordinary household product. And the doctors, like many others at the time, never considered that evil and death might come from within one's own family.

Wythe continued to insist that he was poisoned by his great-nephew, and after Michael Brown died, Wythe decided to change his will. His lawyer, Edmund Pendleton, arrived, as did his friend, Richmond mayor William DuVal. Wythe dictated the terms of the codicil, or addition, to his will. He specifically eliminated George Wythe Sweeney and stated that his estate should be divided among his great-nephew's siblings.

After two days the doctors began to reconsider their diagnosis, since cholera kills its victims within forty-eight hours. This time when they came to the Wythe home, they did search young Sweeney's room and found a mixture of arsenic and sulfur.

Word spread throughout Richmond that the beloved old man was dying and that George Wythe Sweeney was guilty of his murder. Sweeney was arrested, however, not for murder but for forging checks and was placed in jail. The jailor, expecting Sweeney to be bailed out soon, did not search him thoroughly and took Sweeney's word that the bag he carried contained "pennies." Then the jailor's young slave Phoebe reported that she had seen Sweeney throw something out of the jail window. The jailor went with her to the spot and found two pieces of paper with arsenic inside.

Mayor DuVal searched the grounds and outbuildings of Wythe's property and found traces of what he believed to be arsenic on a wheelbarrow. DuVal scraped off a bit of the substance, tested it, and determined that it was indeed arsenic. Two slaves said they had seen Sweeney using a hammer against the metal to crush the arsenic into powder.

Sweeney's trial for forgery was set for early September, and he was kept in jail on $1,000 bond, a large sum at the time.

George Wythe died two weeks to the day after the poisoning, on June 8, 1806. Church bells tolled throughout the city, and the two newspapers devoted the entire front page to Wythe's life and death. His funeral, as lengthy and elaborate as that for a head of state, was set for June 11, after an autopsy. Hundreds arrived for the funeral, and thirty days of official mourning was decreed by the city council.

Sweeney was charged with the deaths of Michael Brown and George Wythe. Lydia Broadnax survived, but her eyesight was severely damaged. Sweeney would be prosecuted by the attorney general of Virginia, Philip Norborne Nicholas. Richmond citizens felt sure that Sweeney was guilty and would hang. After all, there was plenty of evidence, and the autopsy was performed by three eminent physicians who had all known and treated Wythe, before and after the poisoning.

Who would defend Sweeney? Amazingly, two prominent attorneys offered. William Wirt, from Norfolk, was trying to build up a practice in Richmond, and what better way than to demonstrate his ability in a sensational trial? The second was Edmund Randolph, Wythe's own lawyer. Randolph had been mayor of Williamsburg, governor of Virginia, a congressman, a delegate to the Continental Congress and to the Constitutional Convention, the first attorney general of the United States, and then secretary of state. Because of a couple of public corruption scandals in which he was involved, he had made enemies of a number of influential Virginians, and none came forward to help him financially. He needed money, and he needed to redeem himself, so he wanted to defend this case, even though it meant going against his own son-in-law, prosecutor Nicholas.

Moreover, the two attorneys disliked each other. Wirt had written a satire of Randolph that the latter could not forget.

When testimony began, the doctors testified that arsenic *might* have killed Michael Brown, but they could not say for sure. They testified that Wythe's stomach was full of black bile, which was what had killed him. The bile could have been the result of arsenic poisoning, but the doctors could not state that diagnosis with absolute certainty. Foushee, who had been Wythe's personal physician, testified that the judge had suffered from intestinal ailments before his final illness.

In fact, the three eminent doctors, McClurg, McCaw, and Foushee, had done only a cursory and misleading autopsy. They had opened Wythe's abdominal cavity and examined the stomach interior, but not the liver, which would have shown damage if Wythe had died of arsenic poisoning. Dr. McClurg, who was a specialist in black bile and had written a book on the topic, doubtless mentioned excessive black bile as the cause of death to his two colleagues, who did not argue with him.

In testimony McClurg declared that if Wythe had been poisoned by arsenic, he would have died much sooner, but Wythe had eaten food along with the poisoned coffee, and he had vomited some of the arsenic fairly quickly. None of the doctors accepted Wythe's statement that he had been poisoned and did not administer magnesium, which might have mitigated the effects of arsenic if it had been given quickly. During the clumsy autopsy, the doctors performed none of the known chemical tests that would have shown the presence of arsenic without a doubt. McClurg scorned the use of chemistry in medicine.

What about the doctors' finding ratsbane, a form of arsenic, in Sweeney's room? Ah, many people had that. It proved nothing. Sweeney was found not guilty.

What about the eyewitnesses? Lydia Broadnax had seen Sweeney looking at the will and throwing a paper into the fire after putting something into the coffee. Phoebe had seen Sweeney throw a paper full of arsenic out of the jail window, and two other slaves had witnessed him grinding the arsenic.

None of these eyewitnesses were allowed to testify, for all were black, and the Virginia legal system at the time did not allow blacks to testify against whites.

Spectators were stunned. But not William Wirt. He had known of the useless autopsy results. Dr. McClurg had told Governor William Cabell, who had told Wirt, his brother-in-law.

Some of the parties to the trial were guilty of obstruction of justice, incompetence and/or conflicts of interest, but none paid any penalty. Randolph built up a substantial law practice and successfully defended Aaron Burr against a treason charge a year later. Wirt was named U.S. attorney general and served in the administrations of both Madison and Monroe. The three doctors resumed their busy medical practices. McClurg was even elected the first president of the Virginia Medical Society. Foushee had a street named for him, and McCaw became one of the best-known doctors in the nation.

George Wythe Sweeney was tried for forgery but was acquitted because of a loophole in the law, written by George Wythe himself. The forgery law applied only when individuals had been defrauded, not banks. Upon his release, Sweeney fled from Richmond, never to return. He was arrested and imprisoned in Tennessee for horse theft, so he served time in jail, but not for the brutal murder of two people.

CHAPTER 5

SEEKING THE BEALE TREASURE

There are rumors of treasure buried throughout the South, and especially in Virginia—treasure hidden from invading Union armies, or buried ashore by pirates, treasure on Assateague Island, and Mosby's Treasure. The most enduring tale of lost loot is the Beale Treasure.

Somewhere near Montvale, Virginia, at the foot of the Peaks of Otter in central Virginia, a fortune in gold, silver, and jewels lies buried. Or so many people believe. For more than a century, searchers have pored over the coded message that purports to tell the exact location of the treasure. They have bought pamphlets and maps as well as metal detectors and tried various documents and computer programs to break Beale's code.

Information about the treasure and about Thomas Jefferson Beale is intricate, a story within a story, that involves two lucky discoveries, stealth, obsession, trust, and death.

Thomas Jefferson Beale, according to the letters he left for Robert Morriss, was a rootless man, a veteran of the War of

1812, determined to make his fortune in the West. He gathered a group of thirty friends and set out in 1817 from Buford's Tavern, now Montvale, in Bedford County, Virginia, on a hunting expedition. There was a ready market for beaver, buffalo, and bear skins, and the men bade their families good-bye and set out for what they knew would be at least two years away from their homes in Virginia.

At St. Louis they hired an Indian guide and headed for the Spanish outpost of Santa Fe. The group split up and managed to kill and skin a few animals, but one party discovered a rich vein of both gold and silver. For a year, working in shifts, the thirty men dug the ore, cracked and washed it, and accumulated more than a thousand pounds of gold and nearly four thousand pounds of silver. The group was divided: Part wanted to portion out the gold and head home, while the others wanted to keep digging for gold and silver as long as the vein of ore lasted. They decided that Beale and ten of the men would take the bullion back to Virginia, bury it in a secret place near Buford's Tavern, and find a dependable man to entrust with their secret. If Beale did not return within a year, or if the vein ran out, those left behind would break camp and head for Virginia.

So, in 1819, Beale and his group made their way back to Virginia, with a heap of animal skins in each wagon covering the pots of treasure. They found a suitable spot, and—according to his letters—dug a hole six feet deep near a big oak tree and buried the treasure, sealed in six huge iron pots.

While most of his companions dispersed to spend time with their families, Beale and two others went to Lynchburg. There, Beale planned to investigate Robert Morriss, to whom he thought he might tell his secret. Morriss and his wife, Sarah, ran the Washington Hotel. After several days the three concluded that Morriss was well respected and trustworthy. Beale remained in Lynchburg, enjoying social life, while the other two continued to Richmond, where they sold the animal skins.

Beale began to think of a code he might use to disguise his description of the hiding place. Codes were popular in that era. President Jefferson had used code in his communications with explorers Lewis and Clark.

Beale and his companions returned to the Santa Fe area and found that the miners left behind had accumulated another trove of treasure. So, in the fall of 1821, Beale and a new group set out for Virginia with two loaded wagons—again, with their precious metal covered by animal skins.

At St. Louis Beale attempted to get one of the wagons repaired or to buy another wagon. He ended up trading some of the gold and hides for $13,000 worth of jewels, which were much lighter to carry. The group made their way to Buford's Tavern with only one wagon full of treasure, which they again buried in the secret spot. This time they had 1,907 pounds of gold and 1,288 pounds of silver. As before, they worked by moonlight, lowering the pots into the pit. They covered the treasure with rocks and earth and finally with brush and dead leaves to camouflage the hiding place.

Beale went again to the Morrisses' hotel in Lynchburg, where he worked out a code that would lead to the treasure if someone had the key. He wrote out three messages. One was a description of the place, but not why the place was important. Thus, if this message fell into the wrong hands, whoever found it would dismiss it. The second message described the treasure. The third listed the thirty men who had participated in finding and hiding the treasure.

Beale put the three papers, really just a series of unrelated numbers, in a locked iron box and gave it to Morriss. The men's names were in code, he told Morriss, to prevent someone from claiming to be one of the miners and duping Morriss. Morriss was to have a share of the treasure equal to each of the others' share. Beale felt sure that he and his companions would return to the hiding place near the Peaks of Otter and reclaim the treasure. But, he told Morriss, if he did not return within ten years, Morriss was to break the lock on the box and—using a code key Beale would send—decipher the message and distribute the fortune to the deserving men named.

If Morriss should be in poor health, he was to choose someone else trustworthy and turn the box over to him.

Morriss promised to abide by Beale's wishes, and Beale set out for the West. Soon, a letter arrived in Lynchburg from St. Louis, dated May 9, 1822. It read:

Ever since leaving my comfortable quarters at your house I have been journeying to this place and only succeeded in reaching it yesterday. . . . How long I may be absent I cannot now determine, certainly not less than two years, perhaps longer.

With regard to the box left in your charge I have a few words to say, and, if you will permit me, give you some instructions concerning it. It contains papers vitally affecting the fortunes of myself and many others engaged in business with me, and in the event of my death its loss might be irreparable. You will, therefore, see the necessity of guarding it with vigilance and care to prevent so great a catastrophe. It also contains some letters addressed to yourself and which will be necessary to enlighten you concerning the business in which we are engaged.

Should none of us ever return you will please preserve carefully the box for a period of ten years from the date of this letter, and if I, or no one with authority from me, during that time demands its restoration, you will open it, which can be done by removing the lock.

You will find, in addition to the papers addressed to you, other papers which will be unintelligible without the aid of a key to assist you. Such a key I have left in the hands of a friend in this place, sealed, addressed to yourself, and endorsed, "Not to be delivered until June 1832." By means of this you will understand fully all you will be required to do.

I know you will cheerfully comply with this request, thus adding to the many obligations under which you have already been placed by me. In the meantime should death or sickness happen to you, to which all are liable, please select from among your friends someone worthy, and to him hand this letter, and to him delegate your authority.

I have been thus particular in my instructions in consequence of the somewhat perilous enterprise in which we are engaged, but trust we shall meet ere long the time expires and so save you this trouble. Be the result what it may, however, the game is worth the candle and we will play it to the end.

With kindest wishes for your most excellent wife, compliments to the ladies, a good word to enquiring friends, if there be any, and assurances of my highest esteem for yourself, I remain, as ever,

Your sincere friend,

Thos. Jeff. Beale

Morriss put the letter with the box, and when ten years had passed with no word from Beale, he looked for the arrival of the code key Beale had mentioned. No such key arrived. Another thirteen years passed until he finally opened the box in 1845, but he could not decode the numbers.

He put it aside once more. Finally, in the midst of the Civil War and shortly before his death, Morriss divulged the existence of the box to James Ward of Campbell County, Virginia, and gave him its contents, including an earlier letter Beale had written. In it Beale described the discovery of gold and indicated that in the paper listing the names of his companions, their addresses were also given, so that Morriss might locate their families and give them the proper share of treasure.

Morriss died soon after, and Ward set out to decipher the code. He guessed that since Beale had been named for Thomas Jefferson, author of the Declaration of Independence, that document would be the code's basis. He started with the shortest message, numbering the words in the Declaration and then using the first letter of each word. The message of the code thus read:

I have deposited in the County of Bedford about four miles from Bufords in an excavation or vault six feet below the surface of the ground the following articles belonging jointly to the parties whose names are given in number three herewith.

The first deposit consisted of ten hundred and fourteen pounds of gold and thirty eight hundred and twelve pounds of silver deposited November eighteen nineteen.

The second was made Dec eighteen twenty one and consisted of nineteen hundred and seven pounds of gold and twelve hundred and eighty eight of silver; also jewels obtained in St. Louis in exchange to save transportation and valued at thirteen thousand dollars.

The above is securely packed in iron pots with iron covers. The vault is roughly lined with stones and the vessels rest on solid stone and are covered with others.

Paper number one describes the exact locality of the vault so that no difficulty will be had in finding it.

Ward noted that Beale departed from a strict "first letter" pattern three times, using a final *y* and an *x* in the middle of a word.

Ward spent the next twenty years working on the other two documents, to no avail. He tried the Constitution, chapters from the Bible, and Shakespearean plays, though he doubted Beale would have known of the latter or had access to them. By his own account, Ward descended from affluence to penury, neglecting his family and his finances. He concluded that Morriss had given him not an opportunity, but a curse.

He wrote a pamphlet telling all he knew of the treasure and included Beale's letters and the code numbers for the first and third documents and his transcription of the second document. He was giving up the search and leaving it open to others. He arranged with a printing company in Lynchburg to print the pamphlet, which he planned to sell for 50 cents per copy. Unfortunately, a fire swept through the printing plant, destroying most of the pamphlets.

Next N. H. Hazlewood, who lived in Montvale, somehow acquired a copy of the numbers. He was sure that the treasure was on his property, but he was unable to break the code. He eventually turned his set of numbers over to Clayton Hart, who traveled to Lynchburg and talked with Ward. He also verified that there had been a Washington Hotel operated by Robert and Sarah Morriss.

Clayton Hart now took up the pursuit of the treasure. He and his brother attempted to crack the code using many of the same documents Ward had tried, and any others that they thought might have been in the hotel in 1822. They tried numbering the words in reverse, using the second letter of each word, using the last letter, skipping the first word and beginning with the second, then with the third, or using every other word. Nothing worked.

Hart even hired the services of a medium, or clairvoyant. After the man was hypnotized, the Harts took him in a buggy to the former site of Buford's Tavern. From there the group went on foot, along Goose Creek and toward the Peaks of Otter. The medium stumbled about, stopping by a huge oak tree to proclaim, "There's the treasure. Can't you see it?" For the next six hours, the brothers took turns digging, and they eventually struck rock, which they removed, but found no treasure. The medium then declared that they were several feet away from the actual site, but daylight had come and they could dig no more at the time. Returning a few nights later with dynamite, Clayton Hart blasted out a large hole nearby but succeeded only in alarming the neighbors.

The Harts next consulted a man noted for his code breaking during World War I and sent him a copy of Ward's pamphlet. The man worked on the numbers and wrote that he thought it strange indeed that a novice such as Ward could have deciphered the second document. He kept Ward's pamphlet and never wrote to them again, perhaps thinking to find the treasure himself.

For years during the Depression, locals living between Roanoke and Bedford, near Montvale, were sure the treasure lay somewhere underneath their property, and occasionally treasure hunters would show up and dig stealthily on someone's farm, finding nothing of value. During World War II the nation's attention was turned to war, not to the possibility of treasure in rural Virginia.

Then, in 1954, an article about the treasure in *Argosy* magazine stirred interest nationwide and brought a new generation of treasure seekers to the area.

Modern-day treasure hunters use computers in an attempt to crack the code and metal detectors to locate the six iron pots. But nearly two centuries have passed since Beale supposedly buried the treasure. Old trees have died and fallen, and giant trees now grow in what was once meadow. Streams have flooded, and landscapes have changed. Even if the exact location were known, it would probably take a bulldozer to clear the surface and bring up the iron pots.

Does the treasure even exist? Researchers have not found any records of a Thomas Jefferson Beale in Virginia. This in itself is not unusual: In that era, birth certificates were not usually issued; some families had no Bibles where births, marriages, and deaths were recorded; and the census could have easily missed someone as peripatetic as Beale. A family of Beales did live not far from Montvale. By his statements in his letters, Thomas Jefferson Beale never married, had no heirs to leave property to, and owned no land, so he would not have appeared in county records. Men often went west and were never heard from again. Still, if thirty men from one area disappeared, it would seem that more attention would have been paid to their disappearance, especially as some of them were close friends.

But if this was all a hoax, who perpetrated it? Beale—if he existed—had nothing to gain by orchestrating such an elaborate scheme.

All who knew Robert Morriss said that he was an honest man, not the type to manufacture such a scheme to deceive others. At one time he had a grand house on Main Street in Lynchburg and was a successful tobacco merchant, but he misjudged the market price and overbought just before the price fell. He lost everything and had to start over as a hotel manager. If Morriss had planned the treasure hunt, he might have let the message "slip" and then sold the information to others. But he didn't.

James Ward would be the most logical person to have developed the codes and the whole treasure idea. No one actually saw the letters Morriss is reputed to have received from Beale; only Ward's reproduction of them was available. The iron box was supposedly destroyed after Morriss broke the lock and opened it in 1845. If Ward concocted the scheme, the code, and the letters, he was a talented writer, with a good knowledge of American history and the western territories, as well as of human nature. And he went to a lot of trouble numbering the words of the Declaration of Independence and then writing out a message and supposedly "breaking" the code. But what did he have to gain? If he wanted to sell pamphlets, why did he leave them in the printer's warehouse to burn?

Treasure seekers are optimists, always believing that they will find the treasure that has eluded all others. Just often enough to keep hopes alive, a treasure is found at sea.

The Beale Treasure, based on the description of the gold and silver that were buried, would be worth millions of dollars at present prices. Beale told of buying a handful of jewels for $13,000 worth of gold, at 1820 prices. He may have been duped into trading his gold for fakes. He didn't say how many or what types of jewels he bought, so no estimate can be given of their present value.

Treasure seekers have spent perhaps more than $1 million in searching for the riches, considering expenses for travel, camping supplies, metal detectors, and digging tools. Only the merchants who sold or rented these items and the Roanoke Public Library, which over the years has sold thousands of copies of Ward's pamphlet containing the codes, have made any money from the Beale Treasure.

SIDNEY VAUGHT

The fabled Beale Treasure is believed to be buried in
sight of the Peaks of Otter.

Who knows? No one believed that the treasure described in the *Iliad* existed, yet Heinrich Schliemann found it. Perhaps someday a flood will wash away the dirt and expose a heap of gold, silver, and jewels amid the rust that once was six iron pots. Or ground will be cleared for a house or a school or a new road, and there among the debris will be Beale's Treasure. Or someone may break the code and discover just where to dig.

If the treasure exists.

CHAPTER 6

WHO *ELSE* KILLED LUCY?

There was no question that Lucy Pollard was dead. She lay near the back door of her home, her skull crushed. Blood had soaked the ground in three places, indicating that she had attempted to elude her killer, and the murder weapon—a bloody ax—leaned against a tree near the body. Within a few days a suspect was arrested. He fingered three accomplices before beginning to change his story. Who else actually participated in the brutal ax murder on a lovely afternoon in June 1895—and got away with it?

Lucy had lived with her husband, Edward Pollard, in Lunenburg County, a rural area of southern Virginia west of Richmond and just north of the North Carolina line. Lucy was a typical hardworking farm wife of the period. When she was struck down, she had been on her way to the henhouse to set eggs for hatching. The broken eggs, marked with the date "15," littered the ground around her body.

Lucy had no known enemies. In many cases when a woman is murdered, her husband is the logical suspect, but not in this case. Lucy was Edward Pollard's third wife, and the other two had also died. He was the person who found his wife's body, though not at the time he said. Still, he had an alibi for the entire afternoon. He had left Lucy talking with a black woman who lived on the farm, Mary Abernathy, and he had gone to the field to work, with another worker as witness. Later he had sold a wagonload of corn to Mr. Clements and helped him load the wagon, walking near where Lucy lay without seeing her.

Edward came home, expecting Lucy to be preparing supper. Instead, he found her body. He rang the iron bell outside and called out until Mary Abernathy and her husband, Wilson, as well as Mary Barnes and her daughter Pokey ran to find out what was wrong.

Edward felt sure that the only reason someone would kill Lucy would be to rob the Pollard home. The Pollards were known to keep money in the house. He went to check his stash of money and discovered that it was all gone, as well as Lucy's bag of gold coins, worth about $65, two gold bracelets, a gold chain, and a bond. Edward, who didn't trust banks, kept his money locked up at home. He had had $800, in $20 bills, a fortune in those days. With that amount Edward could have bought a good-sized tract of land, even a farm with a house on it. He discovered the box unlocked and the key back in place. Had the killer tortured Lucy to make her unlock the box or tell where the key was?

Later there was some discrepancy about the time of Lucy's death—enough time so that Edward would have had the opportunity to kill his wife and then "discover" her body and call for help—but he had no motive, and there had clearly been a robbery as well as a murder.

The sheriff was twenty miles away at Lunenburg Court-house. Someone went in search of a local deputy, who soon arrived. Word spread and a crowd gathered, some merely curious, some wanting to help. Edward sat in the yard beside Lucy's body all night, and both Mary Abernathy and Pokey Barnes sat nearby, keeping him silent company. In the morning the women washed Lucy's body for burial. Everyone hoped Lucy had died quickly from a single blow, but bruises and broken bones revealed that she had put up a struggle, and abrasions on her neck indicated that she had been choked before the ax finally turned her head to pulp and ended her life.

When Edward was asked which clothes he wanted to bury Lucy in, he went to the chest where Lucy had kept her clothing and said he only saw seven dresses—surely Lucy had more. Had someone also stolen her clothing? But he had paid little attention to Lucy's clothing and could not describe any missing dresses.

The next day a tall, light-skinned black man, Solomon Marable, ordered breakfast in a cafe in Chase City, in the adjoining county of Mecklenburg, a short train ride from the crossing near the Pollard farm. The cafe was run by a black woman, so his presence was not unusual, but his paying with a $20 bill was. The owner didn't have that much money on hand, so she sent her daughter to the bank to get the $20 bill changed into smaller bills. A short time later, Marable went to a nearby store and bought himself a suit of clothes as well as women's and children's clothes. Word of his spending spread, and when he and his wife and two small children attempted to board a train for North Carolina, he was spotted by deputies who were looking for him. He threw Lucy Pollard's money pouch to his wife and ran. He was later found and arrested.

Meanwhile, deputies had arrested Mary Abernathy, who had been sitting on the back steps talking with Lucy Pollard when Edward left to do field work. Mary Barnes helped him in the field. Each woman had nine children. When the deputies asked to search Mary Abernathy's cabin for the money, bracelets, and clothing, she complied. They found nothing incriminating, just a tiny home stuffed with people and their meager belongings. Nevertheless, Mary Abernathy remained under arrest. The deputies also arrested Mary Barnes, her daughter Pokey Barnes, and Ellen Gayle. The latter two just happened to be walking near the house around the supposed time of the murder, on their way to pick cherries at another farm. Various "patriotic citizens," who saw it as their duty to solve Lucy's killing and to see that the killers were brought to justice, spirited the women off to a distant farmhouse, supposedly to prevent their being lynched.

After the women were returned to the Pollard farm, Solomon Marable began to accuse them. He admitted that he had been at the scene of the murder, but he claimed that Mary and Pokey Barnes and Mary Abernathy had hatched the plot and asked him to help them. Then he said that Mary Barnes had stolen the money but had not actually struck any blows. Ellen Gayle was released, as she was not implicated in any way.

The three accused women and Solomon Marable were taken to jail. The newly elected Lunenburg sheriff, M. C. Cardozo, only four days in office, realized that he had a problem on his hands. Only three decades after the Civil War, lynchings of blacks were a regular occurrence, and he didn't want one to happen in his county. He asked the governor, Charles T. O'Ferrall, for one hundred troops to control the crowd. The governor offered fifty, which Cardozo felt were not enough, given the publicity the case was stirring statewide. The Richmond newspapers described it as one of the worst crimes of the century. The governor finally agreed to send seventy men.

The town was packed for the trial, and business boomed. Two hotels were located near the courthouse, and several homeowners ran boardinghouses when court was in session. Food vendors, including local housewives, fed the crowds.

No lawyer wanted to defend Marable, as he had already confessed, and he had little idea of how to defend himself. He told his story, changing the details as he heard other testimony. He admitted that he had held Lucy's hands and throat, thus making himself a partner in the murder, but said that the women had hit Lucy first with a stick and then with the ax. At one point he said the women had blood on their clothing, but at another time, no blood. He concluded by saying that Mary Abernathy gave him two $20 bills and that she was going to hide the rest. Marable was found guilty.

Mary Abernathy was also without a lawyer, and she had never had any previous encounter with the law. Mary, her husband, and their nine children were all law-abiding, hardworking people. Mary was pregnant again. She was an unlikely murderer, but after lengthy deliberation the jury found her guilty, based mainly on Marable's testimony and the fact that she was the last person seen talking with Lucy Pollard.

Pokey Barnes was tried next. She didn't have a lawyer either, but she was feisty and intelligent and managed to get Marable to admit that he had lied. Her reputation was against her, however. Edward Pollard testified that Pokey and his wife had quarreled, when Lucy accused Pokey of robbing her garden. Pokey was widowed and had a five-year-old daughter. She supported herself by doing laundry and lived unmarried with an older man who was also widowed.

During the proceedings, Frank Cunningham, the man in charge of the courthouse guard, had managed to get Solomon Marable's confidence, and Marable told him yet another story, which Cunningham brought to the court. This time, Marable said that a white man, not the three black women, had instigated the murder. The white man had put a gun to Marable's head and demanded that Marable distract Lucy Pollard while he stole the Pollards' money. In the midst of this testimony, a man in the court winked at Marable, and the accused broke off his testimony. The "winking man" was Lucius Pettus, who was not on speaking terms with Edward Pollard after a dispute.

Mary Abernathy was pregnant when she was convicted of Lucy Pollard's murder and gave birth to her daughter in the Richmond City Jail.

Despite this amazing revelation, the testimony was taken as just another of Marable's lies. Pokey was found guilty.

Mary Barnes's trial was very quick. The witnesses she called in her defense were vague. It was obvious that she took no part in the killing, as she was hoeing Edward Pollard's garden in his sight at the supposed time of Lucy's murder, but she might have been the mastermind. She was found guilty of second-degree murder and sentenced to ten years in jail. The other three were to be hanged in September.

Mary Barnes was taken to the state penitentiary in Richmond to serve out her term, while the other three accused were taken to Richmond city jail to await execution. Their photographs appeared in newspapers, especially the newly established black newspaper the *Planet*. The women became celebrities in Richmond's black community, and funds were raised to hire lawyers for them—white lawyers, who would have some clout with white judges and juries. The *Richmond Times* began to question whether the women were indeed guilty or had been wrongfully convicted. Lunenburg citizens were outraged that outsiders dared criticize their decisions.

The evidence in the murder case was problematic, at best. There were no official court reporters or stenographers, and of course no videotaping. A reporter had to write up the testimony the best he remembered it and then ride to the nearest telegraph office to send in his story. It's no wonder that facts were garbled.

Solomon Marable at one point indicated that the "white man with the gun" who had committed the murder was David Thompson, half brother of the "winking man." Lucy had lived with the Thompsons before marrying Edward Pollard, and the Thompsons were in debt, owing money to Pollard as well as to store suppliers. They needed money. Had Lucy recognized Thompson in the act of robbery and been brutally silenced?

As time for the executions approached, Marable was baptized and asked the women's forgiveness for accusing them. Meanwhile, the lawyers petitioned the circuit court in Amelia to overturn the women's convictions and grant them a new trial on the grounds that the jury had not been properly sequestered.

Their request for a new trial was denied. They next went to the Virginia Supreme Court of Appeals. While they awaited the high court's decision, Cass Gregory, one of the "patriotic citizens," went to the jail and told each woman that he would petition the governor to pardon them if they would confess and tell him where the stolen money was. Both refused this impossible request.

Marable was granted a month's reprieve before his hanging. Thinking he would be hanged the following day, Marable had repeated his story of David Thompson's attack on Lucy and his own part, grabbing hold of her hands. Marable said that Thompson really intended to kill Edward Pollard, but since Edward was not home, he settled for killing Lucy. Thompson, son of a prominent family, was the postmaster for Finneywood and brought forth four men who claimed that he had been at his post all day.

Lunenburg authorities attempted to alter the record of the trial to show that the jury had been properly sequestered and admonished not to talk.

Sheriff Cardozo went to Richmond to fetch the prisoners back to Lunenburg on November 8. Governor O'Ferrall feared that the prisoners would be lynched and had troops on stand-by to escort them, but he also feared the political fallout if he used troops without the sheriff's request. Finally he had the troops disband and instead sent word to the jail that the prisoners were not to be released. Sheriff Cardozo returned to Lunenburg angry and empty-handed.

John Mitchell Jr., editor of the *Planet*, had made the prisoners' plight public, and contributions poured in from across the nation to pay for their defense.

Finally the Supreme Court of Appeals ruled on December 12 that the Lunenburg court's decision should be reversed and that Pokey Barnes, Mary Abernathy, and Solomon Marable be granted new trials. Mary Barnes had agreed not to seek a new trial, as her sentence might be heavier if she were found guilty a second time, but instead decided to serve out her time and hope for an early release.

On January 1 Mary Abernathy gave birth to her daughter, Bessie Mitchell Abernathy, in the Richmond city jail. The doctor sent word that she could not travel for several weeks. The other two could, however, and less than a week later Pokey Barnes and Solomon Marable were taken in the dead of night to Lunenburg, heavily guarded by men armed with shotguns. Marable's scaffold still stood, his intended grave beside it. Two weeks later Mary Abernathy and her baby were also brought to Lunenburg. The purpose of this court appearance was to decide if they should be tried again in Lunenburg or elsewhere.

They were granted a change of venue. Their new trials would be held in Farmville, the county seat of Prince Edward County. Like Lunenburg, Prince Edward was Southside Virginia, largely rural with a population of white landowners and poor black workers. However, Farmville had a number of black businesses, and the county boasted a college and a "normal school" where teachers were trained. And to be sure the prisoners were safe, a group of black church members organized and guarded the jail and the local roads every night.

Marable's trial was first, beginning on March 16. He was ably defended by lawyers who asked why there had been no further investigation after his arrest, and why the missing money had not been found. Still, he had confessed to his part in the murder and was again found guilty.

Mary Abernathy's trial was a different story, with new evidence and new testimony. Edward Pollard's testimony established that on the morning of the murder he had threatened to sue one Thompson and had been threatened by another Thompson for taking a shortcut across Thompson property. And Marable had testified earlier that Thompson, the alleged killer, had said he had come to kill Edward but had settled for Lucy. Edward's testimony also indicated that he had only guessed at the time of Lucy's murder. And no one asked why he had not seen her body when he helped load a wagon with corn nearby.

The jury found Mary Abernathy guilty. The defense appealed.

Pokey Barnes was the last to be retried. Edward Pollard again testified, and this time he revealed that he had loaned $100 to another member of the Thompson family just a month before the murder and that the borrower had been unable to repay the loan. Was that a motive for robbery and murder?

A second witness, who had not testified in the earlier trials, admitted that Cass Gregory had asked her to testify. Why was he so interested in seeing the black defendants convicted?

After the prosecution ended its case, and before the defense began, the prosecuting attorney himself asked the judge to dismiss the charges against Pokey. There was simply not enough evidence to convict her. Pokey was finally free. She was smuggled out of town that evening on a train for Richmond. John Mitchell, editor of the *Planet,* met the train and took her on a triumphant tour of the area so that those who had supported her and contributed to her defense might have a look at her.

Mary Abernathy and Solomon Marable, on the other hand, were both scheduled to hang and were taken to a jail in Lynchburg.

Marable was hanged on July 3, 1896, just over a year after Lucy Pollard's murder. The night before his hanging, he repeated his story that David James Thompson had held him at gunpoint, forced him to hold Lucy Pollard down, and asked the names of people who lived nearby. If Marable were caught, he was to name those people—the very women he accused. Marable added more details to his story, details he should have given at first.

His body was taken to the Medical College of Virginia for use in dissection class. John Mitchell Jr. rescued it, had it embalmed, and sent it to Marable's wife, Fannie, in North Carolina for burial.

In early September, Mary Abernathy was granted a new trial, her third, on the grounds that there had been insufficient evidence to convict her. By the time she was brought back to Farmville in mid-September, the charges against her had been dropped. Edward Pollard had died and could not testify against her; nor could Marable. She went to Richmond, where her family soon joined her.

On Christmas Day 1896, Governor O'Farrell pardoned Mary Barnes and five other inmates of the Richmond city jail. Mary's husband and family joined her in Richmond. Pokey Barnes remarried and moved to New York.

Just who killed Lucy Pollard? David James Thompson had an alibi, but others of his family did not. Could Marable have given the wrong first name? What did Cass Gregory know? And who got the money? Solomon Marable paid with his life for $40, but someone else got away with murder and a small fortune.

CHAPTER 7

THE SECRET SEVEN SOCIETY

Little can be said about the Seven Society at the University of Virginia in Charlottesville, precisely because it is so secret.

Secret societies have flourished throughout history, as humans like to think themselves special, knowing or doing things beyond the reach of others. Many of these societies involved secret handshakes, code words, oaths, and special knowledge. Books have been written about such societies as the Illuminati, whether fictional or real, and the Masons have long been recognized as a secret society.

The Seven Society at the University of Virginia is a benevolent group, and obviously a wealthy group, based on the number and amount of donations they have made to the university and its students.

Its beginning is also a secret. Rumor says that it began when only seven of an expected eight men showed up for a card game in 1905. Another possible origin is that two other secret societies at the university, the Hot Feet (later the IMP Society) and the Z Society, were so rowdy and disruptive that the college president called for the formation of a more useful society. The result was the Seven Society.

Prospective members are "tapped" in their junior year and become full members in their senior year. Names of members are not revealed until their death. At that time, a wreath of black magnolias in the shape of "7" is placed at the gravesite. The chimes in the bell tower of the university chapel ring seven times at seven-second intervals for seven minutes, beginning at seven past the hour. A notice of the death and the deceased's member-ship is placed in the alumni newsletter and often in the *Cavalier Daily*, the newspaper distributed to students at the university.

Financial gifts by the society are usually made in amounts ending in seven or made up of sevens, such as $777. Incom-ing freshmen learn about the existence of the society during an orientation meeting. After the usual speeches, the person sitting in the seventh seat of the seventh row is asked to locate a paper attached to the underside of the seat, which will indicate the amount the society is donating to scholarships for that class. The society also supports an annual $7,000 graduate fellowship for excellence in teaching.

Other gifts to the university include the mace carried in ceremonial processions, a plaque in the rotunda honoring university students who died in the Korean War, a memorial to Seven Society members who died in World War I, $7,077 to endow a fund for a music library, $47,777.77 for a film on the university's honor system, and $777,777.77 to the Mead Endowment to award grants so that professors may teach their "dream classes."

Donations are made by means of letters signed with seven astronomical symbols representing Earth, Jupiter, Mercury, Mars, Neptune, Uranus, and Venus. Saturn is omitted. Among the big gifts have been the Seven Society carillon in the university's chapel, donated in memory of deceased society members, and an astounding $1 million given to the South Lawn building fund. This donation arrived in a locked box with a key for the university president to unlock it, as well as a shovel so that the society could symbolically participate in the groundbreaking ceremony.

There are lesser donations, too. One student recalled years later that in the late 1940s his classmate had been bemoaning at dinner that he couldn't pay his $250 rent. When he returned to his room, under his pillow was an envelope with $250 for the rent, signed with the symbols of the Seven Society.

A very dramatic donation was made at halftime of the Clemson football game on November 22, 2008. Bobby Page of 3rd Dimension Productions in Charlottesville parachuted into Scott Stadium dressed in black and bearing a black banner with the Seven Society's emblem. He carried a check for $14,777.77 from the society and a letter challenging students to submit ideas about how the gift could be used for "meaningful and lasting ways to directly impact the University community." Proposed

MATT RILEY

Bobby Page, of 3rd Dimension Productions, parachutes into Scott Stadium at the University of Virginia, delivering a scholarship from the Seven Society.

ideas were to be delivered to the statue of Thomas Jefferson in the rotunda by February 7, 2009. Tucking a written message into Jefferson's arm is the usual way to get in touch with the society.

Page said that the society sent him a letter and a check to pay for his jump as well as the donation instructions he delivered.

Not all members of the society have been students or alumni of the university, but most have been. Some of the most notable members include James Rogers McConnell, who volunteered for the Lafayette Escadrille flying group during World War I; Senator Robert Kennedy; Frank Wisner, head of OSS in southeastern Europe and a planner of the CIA; Admiral William Halsey; Edward Stettinius, U.S. secretary of state; and several University of Virginia presidents.

Whom can the university thank for all this generosity? No one by name. Beneficiaries can only put a thank-you note in the crook of Thomas Jefferson's arm.

CHAPTER 8

THE CURSE OF HALL'S STORE

In the early years of the twentieth century, folks who lived near Green Springs Depot in Louisa County were superstitious about Hall's Store and the area around it. The store seemed to have a curse on it. Many misfortunes had happened there, including three murders and a series of fires.

Hall's Store had a good location, on the Chesapeake and Ohio railroad line from Richmond to Charlottesville. A siding by the depot allowed supplies for the store to be unloaded, and produce from nearby plantations could be shipped to the cities. The depot had a telegraph office, and the store had a contract for handling U.S. mail. The store also had a telephone, a rarity in rural Virginia then. The county seat, Louisa, was a short distance away by rail. Despite its advantages, Hall's Store was an unfortunate place for most of its occupants.

The store and a broom factory were built by John Boston. When he died without a will, legal wrangling among his heirs continued for several years. Finally, his son Channing Boston took charge, leasing the store to George Blake from Richmond. Blake made a profit but soon returned to Richmond with his family because of the "roughness" of the area. In 1901 Roy McKnighton leased the store. His brother was shot and killed after a drunken quarrel there, and his lease was canceled.

Next came Silas and Lewis Yancey. The store flourished under their management, until tragedy struck. Silas went on a buying trip to Richmond, was accidentally overcome by gas in a hotel room, and was taken to a hospital. Lewis arrived to stay with his brother until his death. Unknown at the time, a small-pox victim was lying next to Silas. Soon after his return to Hall's Store, Lewis Yancey came down with smallpox, and the depot and store were quarantined. Rail traffic to Green Springs Depot was stopped, the depot became the detention station for all those who had been exposed to smallpox, and the store became the hospital. Another brother of Lewis Yancey as well as another worker died of the disease and were buried in a plot next to the store.

Lewis Yancey survived smallpox but was wiped out finan-cially. Not only had his store been shut down during the quar-antine, but those confined there had to eat the foodstuffs he had stocked. He sued the county for payment but received nothing. Bitter at his treatment by Louisa County, he moved away.

The owner of the store property, Channing Boston, decided to sell instead of leasing. The buyers were William Richard ("Buck") Dunkum and David Asa ("Acey") Dunkum, who in January 1905 took title to the land, the broom factory, and the store, which had living quarters attached. Acey and his wife Elizabeth ("Lizzie") moved into the store with their two daughters, Mamie and Essie, while Buck built his home across the tracks. A clerk at the store, Victor Hall, was also employed at the railroad depot. Both Dunkum families had infants who died and were buried in the cemetery next to the store, beside the smallpox victims.

Then another murder occurred.

A local resident, Isaac Poindexter, quarreled with a real estate man, T. W. Ross. Poindexter threatened to kill Ross, who went to the magistrate and demanded Poindexter's arrest. The magistrate, who was also the telegraph operator and manager of the depot, deputized George Chewning and Joseph Grady. Chewning, known in the area as a ruffian and petty criminal, hated Poindexter and planned to have Grady ambush and kill him as he walked along the country lane that led from his home to the road. However, Poindexter's son hitched up horses to the wagon and drove his father out toward the courthouse. The magistrate had ordered Poindexter to go to the courthouse and post bond, escorted by Chewning and Grady. As the Poindexters drove away in the wagon, Chewning dropped back and shot, killing the son right in front of the Dunkums' store. This was Chewning's second killing within a year. He was found guilty of first-degree murder and sentenced to eighteen years in jail. Lizzie Dunkum was one of the witnesses to the shooting.

The magistrate was fired, and Victor Hall—soon to be a murder victim—became the telegraph operator and manager of the Green Springs Depot.

The Dunkum families continued to operate the broom factory, hiring a local couple to operate the simple binding machine. They bought and sold pulp wood and other lumber products and had the post office concession, in addition to operating a flourishing retail business. They were envied by their less wealthy neighbors.

Tragedy struck the Dunkums again when Acey died of pneumonia in March 1911. The widowed Lizzie, with her two teenage daughters, left the store to be run by Buck Dunkum and Victor Hall and spent most of the next year visiting various relatives in central Virginia.

At the end of her year of mourning, Lizzie put aside her black dresses and responded to the courtship of Victor Hall. He was twenty-four, and she was thirty-eight. In November 1912 the two were married, and Victor moved into the store's living quarters. Victor and Lizzie had the downstairs rooms, and Lizzie's daughters had rooms upstairs. Despite her honesty in dealings at the store and her membership and work in church, Lizzie was criticized. It was not unusual for a thirty-eight-year-old man to marry a twenty-four-year-old woman, or even a teenager, but Lizzie's reverse situation set tongues wagging. Had Victor married her for her interest in the Dunkums' store?

Then the fires started. In the spring of 1913, the broom factory burned. The wooden building, full of stored straw and finished brooms awaiting shipment, was quickly destroyed.

The following week, while Buck and his wife, Mary, were at church, their house burned. It was daylight, a clear day with no thunderstorms, and no oil lamps or cooking fires had been left burning. It was arson, but who had done it? Perhaps one of the earlier tenants of the store building whose business had failed and who was envious of Buck?

While their home was being rebuilt, Buck, Mary, and their two small children lived with Victor, Lizzie, and her two daughters. There was space enough, but friction developed, understandably, as four adults and four children lived and worked together full time. Buck decided that as soon as he completed his house, he would build himself a store, separate from Victor and Lizzie's. Both buildings were completed before the year was out. Dunkum's Store opened in November 1913.

There were now two mercantile establishments on opposite sides of the tracks. Victor Hall bought out the Dunkums' interest in the store that he and Lizzie lived in, and it was called Hall's Store. Dunkum's new store was twice as large as Hall's.

With the Dunkums now in their own place, Lizzie and Victor took in as boarders two young schoolteachers, Elsie Wood and Mamie Crosson. The Halls also employed a twelve-year-old servant girl, Becky Coates, who slept in the pantry on the first floor. Victor's parents, Nicholas and Ellen Hall, and his aunt

Jennie Hall lived about five hundred yards to the rear of Hall's Store, down a dirt lane. The older Halls got on well with their son's wife, despite the age difference, and treated Lizzie's daughters as their own grandchildren.

On the night of April 15, 1914, tragedy struck again, in double measure. In the midst of a heavy rainstorm, the red glow of fire lit the night. Dunkum's Store was in flames, only six months after its opening.

Victor had been feeling ill for several days and decided not to go out in the rain to see the fire. The Dunkum daughters and the teachers had colds and watched the fire from the front window. Lizzie joined others running to see if they could help. It was too late. The building was soon glowing embers. Buck Dunkum had not even been able to rescue his ledgers. His store and its stock were a total loss, and the insurance company was unlikely to pay off, since this was his third fire within a year. They might even suspect him of setting fire to his own store.

Lizzie returned and told Victor all about the fire. Soon Nicholas Hall came by, and Victor asked him to check the outbuildings to make sure no flying embers had set fire to their property. Nicholas checked, reported that everything was all right, warmed himself briefly by the fire, and said goodnight, about 4:00 a.m.

Lizzie fell asleep and was awakened by voices in the store, then Victor's voice calling, "Oh, Lord, have mercy!" Then a gunshot rang out.

Lizzie jumped up and fumbled in the dark to light a lamp. What had happened? Was an intruder in the store? She ran into the store, calling Victor, but got no answer. Victor lay sprawled between the store counters, bleeding from a head wound. Later, Lizzie was never sure just what she did next. She ran to the door, calling out for Buck. Awakening the young ladies upstairs, she called for Becky, who was nearby. She grabbed a bolster to put under Victor's head and a quilt to cover him.

Buck came and tried to call for a doctor, but the phone line was dead. It had burned through from the fire at his store. He set out on foot for nearby neighbors, the Johnsons. One son rode to the home of Dr. Mays, while the other went to fetch the telegraph operator. Dr. Mays could not come but called another doctor. The telegraph operator sent word to Louisa, and a crowd soon gathered at the store.

Victor tried to turn over, groaned, and gurgled as if he might say something. "Victor knows who shot him," Lizzie declared, but her husband was unable to speak.

Buck noticed a pistol on the counter and picked it up. Elsie Woods, the teacher, said that she had gotten Victor's pistol from the dresser drawer in the Halls' bedroom in case the robber came back. Buck took the pistol with him but later put it back on the counter.

In those days there was no designation of a "crime scene" or fingerprinting of weapons. Bloodhounds were used to track fugitives, but by the time any dogs were brought, so many people had walked around the area that tracking was impossible.

Victor was moved to the bed, and by ten o'clock one doctor had come and gone, and two were in attendance. At 10:10 he was declared dead.

By this time an official group—including the common-wealth's attorney, the clerk of the court, the county treasurer, the magistrate, and a former deputy sheriff—had arrived on the train from Louisa. In addition, Mamie Rosson's father, a member of the board of supervisors, had come to fetch his daughter home from this dangerous place.

Lizzie said that she wanted an autopsy done, and it was performed right in the store, on a counter covered with sheets. There were no powder burns on Victor's skin, which ruled out suicide or homicide by someone holding a pistol against the vic-tim's head. A bruise above Victor's eye, the doctors concluded, was caused by his falling against the counter. A damaged bullet was removed. It had penetrated the back of his skull but had not exited.

Victor's parents telegraphed their older son, Sterling Hall, who lived in Charlotte, North Carolina, to come to Louisa. They also wrote an obituary and arranged for a funeral to be held the following day. The magistrate called for a coroner's jury and assembled a group of neighbors.

Commonwealth's Attorney William Bibb was the first to examine the pistol lying on the counter, after removing the bullets and noting that one chamber was empty. Elsie Wood volunteered that she had borrowed it a month or so before to practice shooting. The members of the coroner's jury each sniffed the pistol and declared that it had not been fired recently. It was therefore probably not the murder weapon.

One of the first suspects was Buck Dunkum. Speculation was that Victor Hall might have burned Buck's store to rid himself of a competitor and that Buck shot him in retaliation. Even Lizzie thought this was a possibility and warned Buck, her former brother-in-law, not to talk too much.

The area soon swarmed with detectives, from the police, the insurance company, and the railroad. The Chesapeake and Ohio Railroad was especially concerned with solving the crime, since Victor had been the station agent at Green Springs Depot for nine years and was the second station agent shot within the past year. One of the railway's agents, Myer Angle, had been in charge of investigating the previous killing, which had not resulted in a conviction. This time he was determined to find and convict a killer. Sterling Hall warned Lizzie that she should get her own detective to ascertain the facts so that the insurance companies would not withhold payment. There were two insurance policies, each for $1,000. Lizzie signed one of these over to Victor's parents and the other went to Victor's estate. The Pinkerton detective she hired was paid with the proceeds of this policy.

In the days following the shooting, Lizzie and her daughters, with the help of Victor's parents, tried to get Hall's Store back in operation. They sorted, cleaned, and dusted, and of course they continued to handle the mail. Buck Dunkum set up a temporary store in the depot. Customers flocked to Dunkum's Store and ignored Hall's Store.

When the grand jury convened on May 11, the Louisa courthouse was packed, and a crowd had gathered outside. Lizzie attended in a black dress, with a heavy black veil concealing her face. Her father-in-law, Nicholas Hall, took her to the court-house and back. Buck Dunkum, still a suspect, was questioned for more than two hours and told to return the following day.

That night the Dunkums were awakened by someone knocking at the door, but no one answered when Buck asked, "Who's there?" His father-in-law went to the door with a pistol and indicated loudly that he would shoot. From an upstairs win-dow Buck saw the figure of a man walking away.

The crowd at the courthouse was even larger the following day. When Lizzie and Nicholas returned to Green Springs Depot to pick up the mail bag at the end of the day, the new station-master mentioned that she had a lot of accumulated freight in the depot that ought to be removed. Buck added that it was tak-ing up the space he needed for his store.

Lizzie sent her servant with a wagon to bring home the freight.

That night the depot burned. The arsonist had struck again.

In the early morning hours after the depot was only glow-ing embers, Lizzie went into the kitchen to begin breakfast and smelled kerosene. There was a glow from under the door of the pantry. When she flung open the door, she saw that a small fire had been lit in the middle of the floor. Lizzie poured water on the fire and called the sheriff. He called detective Angle, who alerted a reporter staying at the same hotel.

The sheriff put Hall's Store under guard, and later when Lizzie and her daughters were moving their belongings to a barn for storage, another small fire was discovered in the pantry. Lizzie was suspected of setting this fire as well as the other one in her pantry. And wasn't it strange that she had moved her freight out of the depot just hours before the depot burned?

This was a slow news time, and reporters arrived from various newspapers, eager for a sensational story. Gossip spread about Lizzie, including a story that she had shot Victor so that she could marry a neighbor, Bill Roberts. Roberts had lost an arm in an accident and most of his remaining hand in another, but he had a car and could drive. He offered to drive Lizzie around to the various appointments she had, but this was no more than he had done for other Louisa County residents.

To the newspapers this was a big development. Two men in Virginia, William McCue and Henry Beattie, had recently been convicted of killing their wives, but both had confessed before their execution, and both had obvious motives. Lizzie, however, had no motive for killing Victor. Everyone who was asked testified that the couple was very happy despite the difference in their ages.

Lizzie was arrested and charged with Victor's murder but was allowed to spend the night with her family in the Louisa jail. She was released on bail on condition that she stay out of Louisa County until her trial, except when she had to meet with her attorney, Lindsay Gordon. The first morning after her release, the attorney took her from boardinghouse to boardinghouse, looking for a place to stay while they prepared for trial, but she was refused lodging everywhere.

When Lizzie got on the train to leave the county, her mother-in-law was with her, which confused the mob that congregated at the train station. Another mob was waiting in Richmond for her arrival, but the two women got off halfway there and were met by Gordon, who took them to his home for safety until he could arrange for Lizzie to visit relatives away from Louisa.

Recognizing that her mercantile business was ruined and that she needed money to pay legal bills, Lizzie arranged for the contents of Hall's Store, including her personal furniture, to be sold. The store building and land she later sold for $200 cash and a small house in Richmond where her daughters could live under the watchful eye of her sister. The family would never return to Louisa County to live.

After a lengthy trial in a stuffy, crowded courtroom, the widow was found guilty, not of first-degree murder, for no one could prove a motive, but of second-degree murder. Several of the jurors thought she was innocent of all charges, but if no verdict was reached, she might fare worse in a second trial.

| MRS. VICTOR HALL | LATE VICTOR HALL |

LIBRARY OF VIRGINIA

Elizabeth Hall, accused of killing her husband, Victor, right.

The evidence was all circumstantial. Lizzie was there in Hall's Store, so she had the opportunity to kill Victor, but she had no reason to kill her husband. Victor's pistol was never proved to be the murder weapon, and at least one witness was guilty of perjury, claiming that Elsie Wood had told him the pistol was fully loaded. She denied saying any such thing, and if this was not the murder weapon, then the testimony was irrelevant. Moreover, gun owners often left the first chamber empty to prevent accidental shootings. If Lizzie were being tried now, her conviction would probably be overturned on several grounds, beginning with the prosecution's refusal to turn over to the defense the report of the Pinkerton detective—which Lizzie herself had paid for—until shortly before the opening of the trial.

Lizzie was sentenced to ten years in the state penitentiary in Richmond, where she was put to work making overalls. The beginning of World War I in Europe dominated the front pages of the newspapers, and Lizzie was thereafter ignored by the press, whose sensational stories had done so much to get her convicted.

Almost as soon as Lizzie's sentence was pronounced, Louisa citizens had second thoughts, and some had never wavered in their support of her. Letters from her attorney, her neighbors, and her father-in-law poured in to Governor Henry Stuart's office. The legislature passed a resolution 54–46 asking the governor to free her. Even the judge who had presided at her trial asked for her pardon and subsequently resigned. Only prosecutor Bibb refused to sign a petition for her pardon or release.

The governor was reluctant to pardon her because of cases elsewhere in which a prisoner was paroled only to be lynched. Also, he thought it was politically a bad idea. His attorney general was planning to run for governor and didn't want to stir up unfavorable publicity regarding Lizzie's trial.

Fortunately, Westmoreland Davis won the governorship. He was moved by the many letters in support of her. On

November 10, 1919, when Elizabeth Hall had served half of her sentence, Governor Davis pardoned her.

Once freed, she got a job as linen matron at Grace Hospital. Her daughter Essie became a stenographer and married a co-worker. Mamie entered law school and married an assistant clerk of the Court of Appeals.

Lizzie lived twenty-seven more years, dying on November 22, 1946. She was buried in Richmond, and her obituary listed her only as "Elizabeth Hall, widow of Victor Hall." In the summer of 1914, she had been the most infamous woman in Virginia. In 1946 her death did not even rate a single article.

So who shot Victor Hall? And who was the arsonist? Eventually the store was torn down. But the mysteries surrounding Hall's Store were never solved.

CHAPTER 9

THE TUNNEL VAMPIRE

The Church Hill Tunnel in Richmond, Virginia, claimed victims from the very beginning. When it was built in 1872–1873, it was an important link on the Chesapeake and Ohio (C&O) Railroad, running from the Midwest to the Atlantic. The tunnel ran under Jefferson Park, through several layers of clay and sand, but most of the hill was made up of soft earth and was subject to saturation and collapse.

During construction, there were nearly a dozen cave-ins, some serious enough to kill workmen, and most were due to insufficient interior support. In one collapse, several houses tumbled into the tunnel.

Within ten years after the tunnel was built, Collis Huntington had extended the C&O line to Newport News, the port on the James River, and had built double tracks on a viaduct along the river, reducing the need for the Church Hill line. It was then used mainly to carry coal to the Richmond city gas works. Then, still later, as traffic grew on the C&O and locomotives were heavier, straining the viaduct, it was decided to enlarge the Church Hill Tunnel and route the heavy equipment that way.

Work was under way on the enlargement when tragedy struck on the afternoon of October 2, 1925. Temporary bracing was in place to hold up the ceiling while overhead bricks and masonry were removed and earth scraped out to enlarge the opening of the tunnel. It had been raining, and the earth was sodden.

Tom Mason, the engineer, took the locomotive into the eastern end of the tunnel, pulling several cars that workmen were to fill with the excavated earth. The train passed under Broad Street and stopped about eighty feet from the western entrance so that the cars could be uncoupled. Suddenly a mass of bricks fell from the ceiling, shorting out lights in the tunnel, and dirt poured in on the locomotive, crushing it. Benjamin Mosby, the foreman, was scalded by steam from the locomotive, and Mason was buried with his engine.

The workmen panicked and ran back out of the eastern end of the tunnel, some disappearing into the crowd. Mosby also ran from the tunnel, burned flesh hanging from his bleeding body. He told the crowd that had gathered to get word to his wife that he was all right, but he wasn't. He died in the hospital that night. One man who ran back into the tunnel in an attempt to save Mason was buried alive with the engineer and several others.

Rumors spread that a vampire had been disturbed in the tunnel and had run out and fled to the tomb of William W. Poole in Hollywood Cemetery. Why Poole's tomb was the vampire's destination is unclear. Poole was an accountant who had died three years before the tunnel collapse.

The "vampire" was probably the hideously wounded Mosby, screaming in agony from his burns, his teeth broken from the impact of brick, and too badly injured to know where he was running.

The vampire legend lives. Though no one has seen him lately, he is said to come from the tomb at random times. There are, however, no photographs to document his sudden appearances.

Meanwhile, efforts were made to free the buried men. A gas leak at the eastern end of the mile-long tunnel made any rescue work there too dangerous. A spark could have set off an explosion. Workers began to remove earth and debris from the western end, but progress was slow. Each yard of excavation had to be shored up with timbers and cross-bracings. A steam shovel brought in to remove earth quickly caused further collapse and was removed.

Finally, nine days after the collapse, workers reached the crushed locomotive and found Mason dead, pinned in place by the throttle.

C&O Railroad executives decided to seal up the tunnel and fill it with sand. The engine still lies entombed within the tunnel.

And the vampire? Was it Mosby? Scalded, bleeding, with broken teeth, he might well have resembled a vampire. Or it could have been another half-crazed worker who had extricated himself from the tunnel collapse and fled, hardly knowing where he was going, toward Poole's tomb in Hollywood Cemetery.

CHAPTER 10

WAS ANNA REALLY ANASTASIA?

For decades rumors circulated that the Grand Duchess Anastasia had survived the terrible fate of her family, and several claimants came forward. The most believable of these was Anna Anderson. Was she Anastasia?

As World War I went into its third year, casualties mounted, and it was clear that Russia was losing to Germany. Tsar Nicholas II, a grandson of Queen Victoria, was forced to abdicate, and for a time Russia had a democracy. Then Vladimir Lenin led an overthrow of the government, establishing the Bolshevik, or Communist, regime. Taking no chances that the tsar might return to the throne, Lenin had the tsar, his German-born wife Alexandra, the Tsarevich Alexis, and the four daughters—the Grand Duchesses Olga, Marie, Tatiana, and Anastasia—arrested and taken to Siberia.

The tsarevich, or heir to the throne, suffered from hemophilia. Uncontrolled bleeding into his joints left him a cripple. Tsarina Alexandra was also crippled due to scoliosis. The family, as well as three servants and the family physician, Dr. Botkin, were kept prisoner for more than two months in a house in the Siberian town of Ekaterinburg, crammed into tiny rooms. The windows were painted over, so they couldn't even enjoy the flowers and forest outside.

Then, on the night of July 16, 1918, people in the Ekaterinburg neighborhood heard gunshots. The following day, the little house was found empty and bullet-riddled, and the royal family, the Romanovs, were gone, but no bodies were discovered.

Word spread that the tsar had been executed but that his family had survived and escaped to the east, in a sealed car on the Trans-Siberian Railway. The next stories included more deaths, but a rumor persisted that at least one of the daughters and possibly the tsarevich had survived, smuggled to safety by a sympathetic soldier.

Soon afterward, the White Army defeated the Reds, or Communists, and began a search for the tsar's family. In January 1919 investigator Nicholas Sokolov was assigned to probe the disappearance and probable deaths of the Romanovs. With the help of two of the tsarevich's tutors, Sokolov found the ruts where carts had carried the royal family's bodies into the forest. He found a few remnants of the Romanovs—charred bones, a human finger, jewelry, teeth, and corset stays. He carried this box of evidence out of Russia to western Europe and in 1924 published a book on the deaths of the family. At that point, the Communists controlled Siberia, so no one could search for the bodies, which Sokolov said had been drenched in acid to dissolve them and dumped into a mine shaft.

Other grand dukes and grand duchesses managed to escape Russia and made their way to various European cities and to America.

Rumors then spread that the tsar had left a fortune in European banks, and various people—in Siberia, Denmark, Arizona, Canada, and England—came forward, claiming to be the missing royals. Two, claiming to be the missing Alexis, later worked for the American CIA, and one, a Polish officer, was eventually given a pension for his services, though he was not proclaimed the tsarevich. It was relatively easy to detect a fake Alexis, by testing the claimant for hemophilia, but it was more difficult to rule out the women who claimed to be the grand duchesses. Still, one by one they were exposed—all but Anna Anderson, who would live out her life in Charlottesville, Virginia.

One winter night in 1920, a young woman jumped from a bridge into the Landwehr Canal in Berlin. A policeman who saw her rescued her. She had no identification papers and would not give her name. She was hospitalized as Fraulein Unbekannt (Miss Unknown) and eventually taken to a mental hospital, where she remained for two years, refusing to talk to anyone.

However, one day she claimed that she was Anastasia, the surviving Romanov grand duchess. She told a harrowing tale of being rescued by a soldier, Alexander Tchaikovsky, who noticed that she was alive amid the dead bodies of her family. He raped and impregnated her, but then he helped her escape to Romania, where she gave birth to their baby and put it in an orphanage. She said she had married Tchaikovsky in the Orthodox Church in Bucharest and that he had been killed soon afterward in a street fight. Investigations found no record of the marriage or of Tchaikovsky's death, but the patient began referring to herself as Anastasia Tchaikovsky and sometimes Anna Tchaikovsky.

Anna said that she had gone to Berlin to seek help from her mother's sister, Princess Irene of Prussia, who was also Anastasia's godmother. She had lost her nerve, fearing she would not be believed, and jumped off the bridge.

Another of the tsarina's sisters, Grand Duchess Olga, rejected Anna's claim, as did Princess Irene, although Princess Irene said that she did see a resemblance to her niece. Why, they asked, had she not sought help from Queen Marie of Romania, who was the tsarina's cousin and who would have recognized Anastasia? Anna refused to answer. Irene's son, Prince Sigismund, living in Costa Rica, did not go to see the claimant but sent a list of questions whose answers only Grand Duchess Anastasia would know. Her answers convinced him. "She is undoubtedly Anastasia of Russia," he declared.

Russian nobility in exile split on whether Anna was Anastasia, but those who believed her gave her help. For the next few years, she lived with a series of families and was periodically hospitalized. Her hosts forgave her imperious behavior, temper tantrums, and forgetfulness, attributing all this to the trauma she had suffered.

They tried to imagine her terror and deprivation. It was no wonder that, while she understood Russian, she seldom spoke it and seemed to have forgotten English altogether. Anna claimed that in Ekaterinburg the family was forced to speak only Russian so that their guards would know what they said, and her last memories of Russia were of coarse peasant language as her family was executed. She could not bring herself to speak the language. Tatiana Botkin, daughter of the family physician who had died with them, believed that Anna's loss of language was due to brain damage.

Anastasia's grandmother, the Dowager Empress Marie, survived the Russian Revolution and went to live in Denmark. She didn't believe that Anna was her surviving granddaughter, but her daughter, Grand Duchess Olga, who was married to a commoner and also living in Denmark, decided to investigate. She sent Pierre Gilliard, former French tutor to the tsarevich and the girls, and his wife, Shura, to Berlin to talk with Anna. They found her in a hospital, near death from tuberculosis of the bone, thin, and hallucinating. They were unable to recognize the chubby girl they had known in Russia in this sick, emaciated woman, but Shura asked to see Anna's feet. Anastasia had had a peculiar knob at the base of both of her big toes. Anna's feet had the same deformation. Shura wept and declared that this was indeed the lost Anastasia. Gilliard wrote the grand duchess, "I can't say for sure that she is *not* Anastasia."

He later changed his mind and wrote a book, *The False Anastasia*, giving lectures about Anna in various European cities.

Grand Duchess Olga, after five letters and several gifts to Anna, also decided that the claimant was probably not her niece.

Others, however, were totally convinced. Grand Duke Andrew, first cousin of Tsar Nicholas, spent several days observing Anna in 1928 and proclaimed that she was indeed Anastasia. His wife, a former ballerina, who had also been Tsar Nicholas's mistress, was convinced as well. Even years later, she insisted that Anna had the eyes of a Romanov, of Anastasia.

Another supporter was Princess Xenia, Anastasia's cousin, who had married an American millionaire, William Leeds, and moved with him to Long Island, New York. Princess Xenia was two years younger than Anastasia and had last seen her cousin fourteen years before, but she felt sure that Anna was Anastasia. Xenia invited Anna to stay with her for six months and, after observing her closely all this time, remained convinced.

The Dowager Empress Marie, Anastasia's grandmother, died in 1928, never having recognized Anna as her granddaughter. Following her death, twelve members of the Romanov family signed a declaration stating that Anna was not Anastasia, but only two of them had actually seen her. The dowager empress's brother, who had been paying Anna's upkeep and hospital bills, was pressured to stop his support.

Prince Ernest of Hesse, Tsarina Alexandra's brother, paid investigators for a German newspaper to prove that Anna was not Anastasia, but rather a Polish waitress, Franziska Schanzkowska. The siblings of the supposed Franziska gathered before

Anna and witnesses but could not declare with certainty that the claimant was their sister. One witness had been paid by the newspaper for her story.

Meanwhile, in Long Island, Anna had quarreled with her cousin Xenia. The pianist Sergei Rachmaninoff arranged for her to live in a hotel suite in New York, where she registered as Anna Anderson, and she then moved in with a wealthy New Yorker, Annie Jennings, who enjoyed the social attention of having the tsar's daughter as a guest. And there was always the possibility that the lost fortune of Tsar Nicholas might be found.

Anna found a new supporter in Gleb Botkin, son of the royal physician and younger brother of her champion, Tatiana Botkin. Gleb had drawn cartoons of animals for the young grand duchesses, and when Anna met him in America, she asked, "Did you bring your funny drawings?" Gleb believed her claim, and would continue to believe it for the remainder of Anna's life. However, he alienated the surviving Romanovs by writing that their callous treatment of Anna was due to greed over the money.

Gleb Botkin hired a lawyer who spent years going back and forth between America and Europe, filing claims for Anna against the Bank of England. His expenses were paid by Annie Jennings and by a corporation set up by her friends. Anna claimed that her father, Nicholas II, had deposited 5 million rubles in the Bank of England for each of his daughters, to be used as dowry. No such deposit was ever found, though Baring's Bank in England did have 4 million pounds on deposit from the Russian imperial government. This was frozen in 1917 and finally dispersed in 1984 to those who had claims against the pre-Communist Russian government. None of it went to Anna.

Annie Jennings paid the expenses for Anna to return to Europe and spend a year in a sanitarium. Then war came. Anna spent the years during and following World War II in Europe, moving from place to place, castle to castle, escaping first from the German armies, then from the Russian Red Army. At the end of the war, a distant cousin gave her a small cottage beside an abandoned military barracks.

Then the play and film *Anastasia* appeared, implying that Anna was the lost Grand Duchess Anastasia. Anna was paid $30,000 from proceeds of the film, with which she built a cottage. When Anna's photos appeared in newspapers, some people said she couldn't be Anastasia—she didn't look at all like Ingrid Bergman!

Scientific studies were made, attempting to determine the truth of Anna's identity. First, all the known photos of the young Anastasia were gathered; then Anna was photographed in the same lighting and from the same angles, and the photos were superimposed. They were identical, the photographers declared. Another study compared the skulls and ears of the two, with the same result: Either Anna was Anastasia or there was a miraculous coincidence of nature. But in the end, German courts ruled that such identification was inconclusive.

Anna's champion, Gleb Botkin, now living in Charlottes-ville, Virginia, continued to look out for her interests. He met a wealthy, unmarried genealogist, Dr. John Manahan, and told him Anna's story. Intrigued, Manahan invited Anna to come to Charlottesville and live in his home. She accepted and in July 1968 flew to Virginia at Manahan's expense. Six months later, the two were married, with Botkin as witness. The frail, bent bride was seventy-two; her groom, a stout, round-faced forty-nine. Anastasia Manahan, as she now called herself, had at last found financial security, and her husband relished the idea that he might be married to royalty. He referred to his wife as the grand duchess and himself as the grand duke–in–waiting or the tsar's son-in-law.

Over the next few years, the strangely matched Manahans traveled around Virginia, attending social events at the Society of Virginia, dining out at the Farmington Country Club and other places, and giving presentations at schools, during which Anastasia talked of her life in imperial Russia. Each day they drove from their stately home on Rugby Road in Charlottesville to his nearby farm, and over the years they adopted a growing collection of stray cats. Despite his money, their home became ramshackle, the garden neglected and filled with weeds, the floors covered with newspapers to absorb cat urine. "It's the way Anna wants it," Manahan explained when visitors pointed out that he could hire cleaning help. Eventually they were taken to court by neighbors who complained of the smell.

Long considered eccentric, the Manahans became paranoid, insisting that they were being shadowed by the CIA and the KBG, that their lives were in danger, that Anna was not just the Grand Duchess Anastasia but also a descendant of Spanish royalty and of Genghis Khan.

In the summer of 1979, Anna had a days-long bout of vomiting and stomach pain but refused hospitalization until she was near death. Then Manahan took her to Martha Jefferson Hospital in Charlottesville, where surgeons discovered a blocked, gangrenous intestine. A foot of her intestine was removed, as well as an ovarian tumor, and tissue samples were sent to labs for analysis.

Anna recovered from the surgery, but her madness grew worse, as did her descriptions of what she and other members of the Russian royal family had endured. In November 1983 she was admitted to a mental institution. Her husband kidnapped her, and for three days the two drove around Virginia, evading an all-points bulletin by the Virginia state police. Eventually they were found, and Anna was again placed in a mental institution, where she remained until she died three months later of pneumonia, on February 12, 1984. Manahan had her cremated and took her ashes to Castle Seeon in Austria.

When Jack Manahan died in 1990, he left his millions to a young lawyer, Althea Hurt, who has carried on the fight to prove that Anna was Anastasia. Manahan was Anna's heir, and Hurt is Manahan's heir. If it could be proved that Anna was Anastasia, then Hurt would stand to inherit not only Manahan's millions but also any of the Romanov fortune that still exists.

The mystery of Anna/Anastasia would have fallen into obscurity but for events that transpired a world away, back in Russia.

In Ekaterinburg, called Sverdlovsk during the Soviet period, Alexander Avdonin had been both fascinated and horrified by the execution of the royal family. Throughout his life he had visited the Ipatiev House, where the executions had taken place. He had talked to anyone who would tell him what they remembered about that terrible time. Then the writer and filmmaker Geli Ryabov came to Sverdlovsk to show a film about the Soviet militia and became intrigued with the events and the setting. In 1977 the two were introduced and joined forces to search for the royal family's remains.

The government had just torn down the Ipatiev House, claiming that it was attracting secret tsarists. But Avdonin and Ryabov had an unexpected gift: The son of one of the executioners gave them a copy of his father's report, describing what was done with the bodies and where they were dumped. He said it was his way of atoning for the "terrible thing."

Avdonin and Ryabov found the site, dug down, and found three skulls. Realizing that it was still dangerous to pursue the truth about the Romanovs, they returned the skulls to the grave a year later, in 1980.

When the Communist government fell in 1989, the Soviet Union broke into separate countries, and the secrets of tsarist and Communist times were revealed. Ryabov went public with the news of their discovery, but it took two more years before a scientific expedition traveled to the site in 1991 and photographed it, observed by Russian officials.

Nine skulls and hundreds of bones were found in the grave, but there should have been eleven skulls, for the eight Romanovs had been killed along with three servants. DNA was taken from members of the British royal family,

Anna Manahan, who claimed to be the Grand Duchess Anastasia, and her husband John. He holds a portrait of Russian tsar Nicholas II, Anastasia's father.

who were cousins of the Romanovs. There was no doubt that these were the Romanov remains. But the bones of the tsarevich and one of his sisters were missing. But which grand duchess? By superimposing photographs of the skulls onto photographs of the Romanovs, it was announced that Marie, not Anastasia, was the missing heiress. However, after further tests, forensic archaeologist William Maples announced in 1992 that Anastasia was the missing grand duchess.

Members of the British royal family declared categorically that Anna Manahan had been an imposter.

There ensued a lengthy series of lawsuits in Virginia over the tissue from Anna Manahan's bowel. Finally, an attorney for Gleb Botkin secured the right to have the hospital release the tissue, and it was tested by two different labs. The conclusion: Anna was not a Romanov.

Rumors persisted that the hospital sample had been switched in transit, as it passed through many hands. Then another sample of Anna's DNA was found. In a Chapel Hill, North Carolina, used book store, a customer bought a book for $100 that had belonged to John Manahan. Inside was an envelope labeled "Anna's hair." Follicles clung to the strands. The sample was rushed to another lab for testing, and ironically it too showed that Anna was not a member of the tsar's family. But was it really Anna's hair? It could have belonged to someone from Manahan's family, or even the book dealer's.

Who was Anna Manahan? The labs just happened to have DNA samples from the family of the Polish-born waitress Franziska Schanzkowska. She had descended from minor Polish nobility who had fallen on hard times and had gone to Berlin to work. The lab announced that Anna Manahan's DNA matched that of the Polish waitress. This finding explained why "Anastasia" could understand Russian but not speak it, and why she could speak German, which the Russian nobility did not use, but could not speak English, which the tsarina had learned from her grandmother, Queen Victoria, and used with her children.

If Anna Anderson Manahan of Virginia was not the Grand Duchess Anastasia of Russia, she was probably the best actress of the twentieth century.

CHAPTER 11

THE MURDERED MAYOR

Just before 7:00 on the night of March 3, 1972, Fred Duckworth bundled up against the chill of the evening, said good-bye to his wife, Gertrude, and left their apartment at Algonquin House in Norfolk for his last walk, one from which he would not return.

It had been ten years since he had been mayor of Norfolk, but every time he drove around the city, he could see the results of his time in office. He had stepped on a few toes and made more than a few people angry, but he had gotten things done. He had a lot to be proud of. He had pushed through construction of the innovative Chesapeake Bay Bridge Tunnel, which joined Virginia's two eastern shore counties to the mainland. It was a tourist attraction and an engineering marvel, spanning the mouth of the Chesapeake Bay, dipping below the water, bridging above it, and dipping again, for eighteen breathtaking miles. And closer by, new tunnels joined Norfolk and Portsmouth, putting an end to the tedious and time-consuming trips across the Elizabeth River by ferry.

He had also persuaded General Douglas MacArthur to donate his staff car and his memorabilia to a museum that had been established in the old Norfolk courthouse. The general was buried there. The MacArthur Museum too had become a tourist attraction. The general's widow, Jean, lived in Norfolk and was a friend of the Duckworths'.

Much more controversial and far-reaching was the mayor's urban renewal effort. Under Duckworth's direction, great swaths of downtown waterfront structures had been flattened by bulldozers, making space for new, high-rise buildings. Several historic houses and other buildings were saved, were registered with the National Register of Historic Places, and became tourist attractions, just like the museum and the bridge-tunnel. Sometimes there weren't any developers ready to build on the vacant space, and some plots of land became weedy eyesores. Still, he reasoned, in the long run it would work out for the best.

Norfolk had long been a second-rate city, derisively called the "armpit of the East Coast." It was a port city, the terminus of coal-carrying railroads, and a navy town where sailors on leave could patronize tattoo parlors, prostitutes, and seedy bars. Duckworth wanted to change that image. His vision was for a city that would be respected and that would attract investors, and he had seen it come to pass. Annexation had doubled the city's size, making it bigger than Richmond, the state capital, and it had earned the designation All-American City. But homeowners, renters, and small businesses displaced by the "renewal" were angry.

Then there was the matter of the schools. Closing the schools to stop integration had angered many citizens, especially the parents of children who missed out on an education because of Duckworth's decision. For a time, Mayor Duckworth had closed the largest white high school to prevent seventeen black students from enrolling. This left the black schools in operation. Then he decided that his action was penalizing white students and rewarding blacks, so he closed all public schools until the Supreme Court ruled that schools must be integrated. Those who would have entered high school in Norfolk in the fall of 1955 were referred to as the "lost class of 1959." They had a reason to resent the former mayor.

So, Fred Duckworth was revered by some but reviled by others.

And someone wanted him dead.

The former mayor varied his walks somewhat each night, but he went out at approximately the same time, and his route almost always took him past Powell Pharmacy on Little Creek Road. While there, he would call his secretary, Ruth Hodges, from a pay phone. He called her as usual on the night of March 3, "checking in" that he had reached the halfway point of his walk.

Shortly afterward, at 7:50 p.m., a motorist, Jesse Moore, was returning from buying groceries at a store on Little Creek Road. As he turned onto Major Avenue, his headlights picked out the form of a man lying by the sidewalk in a vacant lot. He stopped and went over to the fallen man, touching his neck. The man was still warm. He was probably still alive and needed medical help. Moore ran to a nearby house on Major Avenue, knocked on the door, and told Anna Ritter about the body. She called police.

Within minutes Detective Ralph Mears arrived. At first he thought the man on the ground had died of a heart attack. The victim lay on his back. His hat and rolled-up umbrella lay nearby. He still wore glasses, though they were pushed up on his head. He had gray hair and a slightly slack face, not unusual for a man who looked about seventy.

Several other patrolmen were on the scene, making arrangements to transport the man to a hospital. A neighbor walked up and identified the fallen man as former mayor W. Fred Duckworth. The victim's importance put the case in a different light. Then one of the patrolmen found some shell casings. The mayor had not had a heart attack; he had been shot, more than once.

An ambulance took him to a hospital, where he was pronounced dead. His body was taken to the state crime lab. The Duckworth shooting was now a high-profile murder case.

The location of the seven shell casings found with the mayor indicated that someone had fired at him from close range and on foot. It was not a drive-by shooting. Was it a robbery gone wrong? The bent umbrella could mean that the mayor had put up a fight. But his coat was still buttoned to the chin, his pockets had not been turned out, and he still wore gloves that concealed valuable rings. His wallet was missing, but when his wife was notified of his death, she said he never took his wallet on his nightly walks.

So, was it a random shooting? Who would shoot an unarmed seventy-two-year old man? The detectives realized that the crime was a grudge killing, probably by a paid hit man, and obviously a well-planned murder. Someone had observed the mayor's nightly walks and knew just where he went, and when.

The location of the shooting, close to a major thorough-fare, was well chosen. The body was sure to be found, but the killing was not likely to be observed. No houses faced the vacant lot where he had fallen, which was rimmed by trees that cut off the view from the busy street. Across Little Creek Road were a professional building and a school, both closed for the night, and apartments that faced the other direction.

Several neighbors who were questioned said they had heard noises like a car backfiring about 7:45 p.m.—shortly before Moore discovered the body—but when they looked out their windows, they saw nothing. The time of year was also a factor in concealing the murder. It was already dark by 7:45 on March 3. Moreover, the site of the murder was near Titustown, an unsavory area. Few residents of Major Avenue or Little Creek Road would have been out walking on the residential street after dark—only the former mayor and his killer.

The autopsy showed that Duckworth had been hit seven times by bullets from a .22-caliber gun, one of which only grazed him. One shot hit him in the back and went through his liver, exiting from the right side of his chest. The fatal shot entered the left side of his chest and tore a four-inch hole in his heart. The bullet was lodged in the right side of his chest. Two other shots broke bones in his right arm, one tore through his left arm, and one was embedded in his buttocks. The shells removed from the body had all come from a single gun, which indicated a single shooter. Had the killer circled the doomed mayor, or had the mayor turned, attempting to evade the shots?

As the story went out over the wire services and appeared in newspapers and on television and radio throughout the region, praise for the mayor poured in, along with anguished questions. If the longest-serving mayor in Norfolk's history could be gunned down, how could ordinary citizens feel safe? The public pressured the Norfolk Police Department to find a killer—and quickly.

Detective Mears was joined by Mario Asaro in the investigation of this high-profile murder. Both were experienced officers and were familiar with the neighborhood where the murder occurred. They fully expected to break the case. Someone had probably witnessed something that he or she didn't consider important but that might be a clue, such as the make and color of a car. And criminals find it just as hard to keep secrets as ordinary people do. A careless word here and there would lead the detectives to their killer, they thought. And perhaps a reward would bring out informants.

Detectives first talked with Gertrude Duckworth, the mayor's widow. She confirmed that he walked five miles each day because of a heart condition, usually breaking his walks into two parts, one during the day and one after dinner. He carried a tear gas pen, but it had not been used. The mayor had thus been surprised by his assailant.

Detective Mears interviewed Ruth Hodges, whom Duckworth had called minutes before his death. She had been his secretary at the Tidewater Virginia Development Council and was executive secretary and corporate treasurer of the MacArthur Memorial Foundation. Duckworth had been concerned about Ruth Hodges's safety, since she had seen a man stalking her, and she was worried after learning that someone had thrown rocks at him the previous evening.

When detectives checked out the phone booth, they learned that someone had been shooting nearby shortly before the mayor's murder. The detectives found the spent cartridge of a .22-caliber gun and a box that had held cartridges.

Soon after midnight there were reports of shots being fired near the 7-Eleven on Little Creek Road, close to the site of the mayor's murder. Detectives saw a group clustered around a phone booth there. The group scattered at the policemen's approach but left behind a pistol: a semiautomatic MAB .22-caliber. By morning the police had arrested several members of the group, and the gun was on its way to the FBI lab in Washington, D.C. The detectives thought they had solved the case.

But they were wrong.

The FBI report stated that the gun found on Little Creek Road could not have been the murder weapon but instead was a semiautomatic made by Sturm, Ruger & Company. So the detectives sent out bulletins to other police departments to be on the lookout for that make of gun. Eighteen months later, they learned that another make of gun—a Browning—could have been the murder weapon. During those eighteen months, various weapons used in other crimes passed through the Norfolk Police Department and were ignored as the possible murder weapon when one of them might have been, if the police had only known to check. This slip-up in communications may have been responsible for a murderer's walking free.

Homicide detectives then were operating in what might be considered "the dark ages" of forensic science. DNA matching was not yet available; the Norfolk Police Department had no facilities to analyze hair or fiber samples; and fingerprint analysis was slow, done by a person visually comparing samples, not by high-speed computers that can search databases from around the world in a few seconds.

Mayor Duckworth's murder made headlines across Virginia and in other states. He was well known in government circles. Besides being Norfolk's longest-serving mayor, he had served on the Chesapeake Bay Bridge and Tunnel Commission, the Virginia State Highway Commission, the Tidewater Development Commission, and the MacArthur Memorial Foundation. Accolades poured in, praising him for his years of service to the Commonwealth of Virginia. His funeral at St. Andrew's Episcopal Church was attended by Governor Linwood Holton; former and future governor Mills Godwin; Jean MacArthur, widow of the general; U.S. Congressman G. William Whitehurst, who read a memorial tribute into the *Congressional Record*; and hundreds of ordinary citizens. His funeral cortege stretched for more than a mile.

On the morning after the murder, a local newspaper headline read "No arrest yet in Duckworth slaying." However, it had been less than twenty-four hours since he was struck down.

A reward was offered for information leading to the identity and conviction of the killer. It started at $5,000 and within a month grew to $10,000, but it lay unclaimed.

Detectives began to sift through Duckworth's life, looking for clues as to who was most likely to want him dead.

W. Fred Duckworth was born in 1899 in Brevard, North Carolina, a small town in the mountains. After high school he attended Davidson College but left after a year and a half to serve in the army in World War I. Returning at war's end, he worked for Ford Motor Company, first for a local dealership and then in the assembly plant in Charlotte. By the age of thirty-two, he was supervisor of the plant.

Duckworth and his wife, Gertrude, had a daughter, Betty. The Duckworths moved to Memphis, where Fred supervised another Ford plant, and in 1936 he was transferred to Norfolk. When war came again, Duckworth became a member of the

The Virginian Pilot

The funeral of murdered former Norfolk mayor, W. Fred Duckworth.

War Production Board. At war's end, recognizing Americans' pent-up demand for new cars, he bought a Ford dealership in Norfolk. He named his dealership Cavalier Ford and ran it with a firm hand, making a fortune in the process.

In 1950 Duckworth began his twelve-year stint as Norfolk's mayor. During that time four hundred businesses and more than four hundred homes in downtown Norfolk were razed, some of them over a century old. A World War II housing project of 2,600 homes was destroyed to make way for an industrial park, and thirty-seven acres of housing were razed to allow the shipping facilities at Lambert's Point to be expanded. What was good for the city's future angered the residents who were displaced. Forcing twenty thousand people to move creates a lot of enemies.

He had also made enemies of the citizens of Virginia Beach. When Princess Anne County proposed becoming the city of Virginia Beach, Mayor Duckworth opposed it and threatened to cut off the water that Norfolk sold to the resort area. Virginia Beach incorporated anyway, becoming the largest city in Virginia and preventing any further annexation by Norfolk toward the sea. There were hard feelings, but hardly grounds for murder.

Tips poured into the police department, keeping Detectives Mears and Asaro busy. Some were vague, some far-out, but none could be ignored. The reward grew to $20,000, but still no one had provided a sufficient lead for an arrest. Mears called in men he had used as informants in the past, men who would tell him the truth for a pittance, much less for $20,000. His informants assured him that blacks had not done the killing.

But who had?

The detectives next turned their attention to the mayor's son-in-law, Phillip Farrand, whom Duckworth had taken into the Ford dealership and eventually made president of the company. Although the two men didn't get along well, Duckworth had sold the dealership to Farrand in 1971, and the mayor's estate was owed more than $150,000. Farrand was an active, upstanding citizen, with no blemishes on his record, and not the kind of man to gun down someone in the street. Nor did he have a motive. Killing his father-in-law would not wipe away the debt or bring his wife an inheritance. Betty would inherit the Duckworth fortune only when her mother died.

So, another possible murder suspect was eliminated.

What about Ruth Hodges, whom the mayor often called on his nightly walks? She would have known his whereabouts at the time of the killing. However, in his various board memberships Duckworth had depended on her accounting and had sent extra work her way. Hodges had no motive to kill Duckworth, and her name was taken off the list.

What about a random killing?

Six months after the mayor's murder, the Norfolk police got a call from Pennsylvania. A hitchhiking soldier had pulled a .22-caliber handgun on the driver who had picked him up. The soldier, Jack Reale, had been stationed at Fort Monroe, across the James River from Norfolk. He had confessed that he had randomly killed men in Ohio and Virginia, choosing his victims because they were alone and vulnerable. He seemed to fit the profile of Duckworth's killer, but when Mears questioned Reale, he denied killing Duckworth. Moreover, he was certifiably insane and was sent to Virginia's Central State Hospital in Petersburg, where he remained for the rest of his life.

Detectives theorized that Duckworth had been the target of a paid killer, a hit man. But who had paid, and who had pulled the trigger seven times? The shooter had chosen a fairly quiet, easily hidden weapon and was a crack shot with the pistol, hitting the mayor—who was moving, attempting to protect himself—seven times out of seven shots.

Time passed, and both Mears and Asaro retired, regretting that they had not been able to find the mayor's killer. Gertrude Duckworth died in 1980, and Betty inherited more than $1 million. Both Betty and her husband, Phillip Farrand, died in 2004.

That year, there was a break in the case—or at least, there appeared to be.

Willie Creedle, a prisoner at the Butner, North Carolina, facility, and originally from Mecklenburg County, Virginia, wanted to talk to the Norfolk police. He said that in the 1970s, when he was living in Virginia, he knew a man named Johnnie Ozlin, who had bragged about killing Fred Duckworth. Ozlin described the killing, but all the details he gave had been published in newspapers. One reason Creedle believed Ozlin's story was that the former marine had arrived back in Mecklenburg County driving a new Porsche. Was that part of his pay for killing the mayor?

Creedle said that he told state troopers about Ozlin in 1983.

The Norfolk detectives discovered that Ozlin's name was in their files as a "person of interest," but there was no record of his ever being interviewed. And he will never be. He had died before Creedle talked to the Norfolk detectives, so he can never answer any questions. Did he shoot Fred Duckworth? If he did, who paid him?

The answer will very likely remain a mystery.

CHAPTER 12

SASHA: SUICIDE OR MURDER?

On the gloomy afternoon of November 7, 1975, Alexandra ("Sasha") Bruce Michaelides lay beneath a tree at her ancestral home, Staunton Hill, in Charlotte County, Virginia, unconscious from a gunshot wound.

Sometime after 4:00 p.m., her husband Marios Michaelides beat at the door of a Staunton Hill employee, Meg Tibbs, claiming, "Sasha's killed herself! She's dying. Call a doctor."

Tibbs called the Brookneal Rescue Squad and ran with Marios through the misting rain to where Sasha lay in a pool of blood. Sasha was still alive, as Tibbs determined by lifting the heiress's limp, warm hand.

Marios went to the mansion for a blanket and returned after a long time with a flimsy covering. Tibbs fetched a quilt from her own house and spread it over Sasha. About 5:00 p.m., Sasha's godmother, Priscilla Jaretski, and a friend came for an expected visit, and a few minutes later the rescue squad arrived at the isolated Virginia plantation.

As Sasha was lifted into the ambulance, someone discovered a pistol beneath the quilt and handed it to the ambulance attendant. As he took it, he noticed that the safety was on. If she had shot herself, there was no way she could have put on the safety or tucked the gun beneath herself so that it would not have been immediately seen by Tibbs.

The ambulance raced to a hospital in Lynchburg, forty miles away, and Sasha's parents and brothers were called. Hospital staff were certain that the gunshot wound to the right side of her head would be fatal, but they were also curious about the bruises on her face and body. It appeared that she had struggled and been beaten before the shot was fired. Records showed that she had been admitted once before with suspicious bruises and had refused counseling.

Police drove Marios back to Staunton Hill and questioned him. He gave three versions of how Sasha had gotten the bruises: She had thrown herself down the stairs in a suicide attempt several days before; she had struggled with him over the gun before shooting herself; and finally, he had struck her and "slung" her. This last remark should have gotten him arrested for assault, but it did not, perhaps because of the prominence of the Bruce family.

Sasha lingered for more than a day, finally dying in the early hours of Sunday, November 9. Her adored father, Ambassador David K. E. Bruce, sat by her side holding her hand until the last. This was the second daughter he had lost in traumatic circumstances.

The Bruces were among the group called FFV—the First Families of Virginia. The ambassador's great-grandfather was the third-richest man in America in the early 1800s and bought thousands of acres of land in Charlotte County, Virginia. His son Charles Bruce was the richest man in Virginia and wanted a suitable mansion. Staunton Hill is the result. Of stucco with crenellated towers, it is unlike the usual Virginia mansions of red brick with white columns. By the time it was completed, the cost had doubled the architect's original estimate, and indeed the house was grand.

The Civil War left the Bruces destitute. Charles's son William Cabell Bruce became a lawyer and a member of the Maryland legislature. His son, David Kirkpatrick Este Bruce, Sasha's father, spent summers at Staunton Hill. In 1914 he went to Princeton, but when America entered World War I in April 1917, he enlisted. When the war ended, he studied in France and became a diplomatic courier.

David envisioned returning to Staunton Hill and living the life of a country gentleman, but his father sold the plantation because it was a financial drain. David became a lawyer, and in 1924 he was elected to the Maryland legislature. After his father was elected to the U.S. Senate, the family spent most of their time in Washington, D.C.

Here David met, courted, and married Ailsa Mellon, daughter of Andrew Mellon, secretary of the treasury and one of the richest men in America. Andrew Mellon gave his daughter $10 million and his new son-in-law $1 million.

David invested his money well and served on the boards of more than twenty corporations. David and Ailsa had a daughter, Audrey, in 1933, and soon after Ailsa bought Staunton Hill back as a gift for David. He spent much of his time in Virginia while Ailsa stayed in New York. David gave funds to build public libraries in Charlotte and the adjoining counties.

By the time World War II began, the marriage was essentially over. The two were too different. David went to Europe, first in charge of the Red Cross in England and later as one of the original members of the Office of Secret Service, forerunner of the CIA. Here he met the beautiful Evangeline Bell, and the two fell in love, though Bruce was twenty years her senior. Ailsa eventually agreed to a divorce in April 1945, and David and Evangeline were married a few days later.

The following May their daughter, Alexandra—who was always called Sasha—was born. David had hoped for a son who would live at Staunton Hill and carry on the ancestral tradition. But Sasha loved Staunton Hill as much as a son might have. She reveled in the time spent there as a child, when she could have her parents' attention, doing the traditional things that ordinary families did. Soon she had two younger brothers, David Surtees Bruce and Nicholas ("Nicky") Bruce.

But the time at Staunton Hill was fleeting. David Bruce was put in charge of the Marshall Plan in France and England, and in 1948 the Bruces sailed for Europe. He was headquartered in Paris. The post was a challenge for David and left little time or attention for his children.

He next became ambassador to France, which meant nightly dinners and other events, often lasting until 4:00 a.m. Evangeline was a talented, lovely hostess and tried to fit the children in by having tea with them each afternoon.

In 1952 the Bruces returned to Washington, where he became undersecretary of state. He was again sent to Europe, this time as temporary special representative to NATO. At Christmas 1954 the family was finally at home at Staunton Hill.

Bruce next became ambassador to West Germany and in 1961 ambassador to the Court of St. James, the official name for the British embassy.

The Bruce children were sent to American boarding schools. Sasha was a good student, high-spirited and likable. She was tall, willowy, and attractive, with long dark hair. She easily made friends who would be loyal to her for the rest of her life. At school she developed a crush on one of the teachers, a married man. He was both the father who had time to listen to her problems and the fantasy lover who could never be matched by the young men she dated. The challenge of winning a married man away from his wife was to be a pattern in her relationships. When she invariably failed, it made her feel less worthy yet more determined to succeed.

Sasha attended Radcliffe during the turbulent 1960s and became involved in sex and drugs. She talked of death and suicide and predicted that she would not live past thirty; however, many children of the 1960s were like that. Sasha promised her godmother, Priscilla Jaretski, that if she ever considered suicide, she would call her. No recluse, Sasha went on archaeological digs, had a special interest in medieval art, camped out with friends, dated widely, and worked at Lyman House, a home for delinquents. She talked idealistically of gathering her friends at Staunton Hill and turning the plantation into a commune for troubled youth.

Everyone's life has some "what if" points. What if she had married Bear Barnes, the handsome, socially connected, wealthy grandson of J. P. Morgan? The two dated for a year and a half, but her friends said that he was too normal and too available to appeal to her.

In 1967 Sasha's half sister, Audrey, and her husband, Stephen Currier, died when their small plane disappeared during a flight in the Virgin Islands. The father of Sasha's best friend committed suicide, as did a family friend, Phil Graham. Death seemed to haunt Sasha.

Sasha's senior thesis was on fifteenth-century illuminated manuscripts and icons, and she did such an excellent job that she graduated *magna cum laude*. She went on an archaeological dig in Israel and toured India, Nepal, and Sikkim. She seemed unable to settle down to any one person or activity. She made several half-hearted suicide attempts, driving her car off the road, and agreed to psychiatric counseling, but she terminated it after a few sessions when she was told that it meant years of therapy in Cambridge.

What was she to do with the rest of her life? Art intrigued her. During a visit to her parents in London, in the British Museum she met a Greek man who called himself Anton von Kassel. He ran the New Grecian Gallery in an upscale part of London, specializing in Greek icons. He had been expelled from his country and was married. Sasha fell in love with him and took his marriage as a challenge. Surely he would give up his wife for her. He did indeed keep his wife out of the gallery they had established, and he installed Sasha as manager. By then, Sasha had turned twenty-one and could draw on a huge trust fund that had been growing throughout her childhood and teenage years. She and Anton moved in together, and he took advantage of both her money and her knowledge of art, especially icons. Soon she was going on buying trips to Greece, smuggling out ancient icons that were not supposed to leave the country. She had an easy way with customers at the gallery, intelligently discussing art and especially icons. Her accent and manner added class, and she was good at sales.

The gallery flourished, but not enough to keep up with Anton's flamboyant lifestyle, which included supporting his wife and child. Besides bouncing checks and lying to clients, he was selling fake icons along with the real, illegal ones, and fake as well as authentic paintings. He was sued by a duped customer, and he forged three checks on Sasha's trust fund. She discovered the deception when the bank called. Nonetheless, she let it go, saying she had approved the transaction.

Anton got a divorce, but instead of marrying Sasha, he began having affairs with other women. Sasha now feared and disliked him but couldn't seem to break free. And how could she prove that he alone had carried out the fraud at the art gallery, that she had nothing to do with the fakes?

Perhaps if she could go to Staunton Hill, things would be different.

Staunton Hill had been owned by Audrey Bruce Currier and then purchased by her father, David, who made a gift of it to his wife Evangeline. The contents, Bruce family items, were owned jointly by Sasha and her brothers David and Nicky. Evangeline wanted her three children to buy the estate from her. Late in 1973, Sasha and Nicky visited their parents in China, where David was again representing the United States in a foreign country, and agreed to their mother's terms of sale.

Shortly before Sasha's trip to China, the gallery in London burned, the fire having allegedly been set by thugs that Anton had hired. He collected the insurance but did not repay Sasha for all her contributions. Instead, Anton asked her to go to a wedding in Greece as his representative, since he was not allowed into his country. She agreed, and there she met Marios Michaelides. He was married, to an American teacher, Mary Lewis, though he didn't tell Sasha that for a long time. He pursued the heiress, claiming that he too was wealthy, the older son of industrialists. She told him about Anton and began an affair with Marios. He seemed the man of her dreams.

Sasha envisioned a simple rural life with Marios, as soon as he could arrange to join her in America. She returned to Staunton Hill, where she began several agricultural projects. She had trees cut and pasture planted, intending to raise cattle. Neither of these projects got very far, but she did raise chickens and sell eggs to stores and restaurants in the nearby town of Brookneal. She had little in common with her neighbors, but she tried to fit in and made a few friends in town. Meanwhile, she was sending loving notes to Marios and calling him on the phone. When a woman answered at the Athens apartment, Sasha discovered that Marios had a wife. But he said he would divorce her so that he and Sasha could soon be married.

Marios demanded to know everything about Sasha's past and beat her until she told him. He then used the information against her, taunting her and calling her a slut and a whore. He said he could not take her to meet his mother in Greece until Sasha was "purified," and that meant repentance and more beatings. After coming to live at Staunton Hill, he had her under his control. He took money from her and bought stocks; he then sold them and transferred the money to a Swiss account in his name only. Recognizing that many of the books in the Staunton Hill library were rare volumes, he sent some of them to dealers for appraisal. He listed some with Sotheby's for sale and had the proceeds deposited into his Swiss account. He even persuaded Sasha that she should not have property in her name, as she had been a partner with von Kassel and might lose everything in the continuing lawsuits against the gallery.

Sasha began a lawsuit of her own, attempting to get some icons that Anton had given her as collateral for a loan but had kept in the gallery.

Sasha's friends couldn't understand her attraction to Marios. He was a chain smoker, prone to migraines, and given to tantrums, but she tried desperately to win his love. He kept Sasha isolated from her family and friends, saying this was the only way she could be "purified."

Marios's wife, Mary, said she would give him a divorce if he would impregnate her, which he did. The two flew to the Caribbean for a quick divorce, and on August 8, 1975, Sasha and Marios were married in a civil ceremony in the Charlotte County courthouse. Marios persuaded her to make a will leaving him everything if they were still married on the day of her death.

Sasha gave Marios a Jaguar as a wedding gift, and they had it shipped to Europe with them four days after the wedding, intending to drive across the continent to Greece. During the cross-continent journey, the car was wrecked in an accident. Sasha bought another Jaguar, and they continued on their way, but Sasha was unhappy. Marriage had changed nothing. Marios was still abusive. They had planned to stay in Greece until

Christmas but instead returned to Staunton Hill in October. In Brookneal she was seen with bruises and black eyes.

Sasha was delighted when her godmother called from Richmond on November 6 to say that she and a friend would visit Sasha the next day at Staunton Hill. Sasha baked a cake, decorated the mansion with flowers, and chose the best champagne from the wine cellar to serve her godmother. This was not the mood of a woman who planned suicide.

After Sasha died early on Sunday morning, her parents, her brothers, and Marios arranged for a private burial at Staunton Hill. Sasha was not embalmed, nor was there an autopsy. Under Virginia law, if a corpse is buried within twenty-four hours of death, there is no requirement for embalming.

Sasha's parents returned to Washington, and her brothers stayed on for a while at Staunton Hill. Marios discovered that much of Sasha's wealth was not hers to bequeath and demanded $600,000 from the brothers to renounce all claims to her estate. They offered him $190,000, which he accepted.

Marios reunited with Mary, who had just given birth to their daughter. He returned to Staunton Hill twice with a car and trailer and left with items he claimed were his, including Bruce family silver. The Bruces hired a detective, who traced Marios to Tennessee, and he grudgingly returned some of the silver. After an inventory of Staunton Hill showed that some paintings and rare porcelain were missing as well, the detective and the police went back to Marios and Mary's apartment, but

LIBRARY OF VIRGINIA

Staunton Hill, the ancestral Bruce home,
where Sasha Bruce Michaelides was shot.

he was gone. In their presence, Mary called Athens and told Marios not to return. Armed with a search warrant describing particular items, the police later seized cartons of Bruce property ready for shipment to Greece.

The Charlotte County commonwealth's attorney, Edwin Baker, drew up charges against Marios for murder, theft, and bigamy; the latter charge was brought because he had not been legally divorced when he married Sasha. Baker asked Greek authorities to return Marios, but they refused. They would try him if Baker would send all the evidence to Greece. Eventually he did, but he could not afford to pay for witnesses to go to Greece to testify. Marios was quickly acquitted.

A broken-hearted David Bruce died two years after his daughter.

David Surtees Bruce, Sasha's brother, brought civil suit against Marios for theft and wrongful death and went to Greece for the trial, but the result was the same. Marios claimed that Sasha had given him money and that she had been abused by her family, not by him. She had several times attempted suicide, he said, and after he had saved her, he had destroyed her notes.

Marios Michaelides refused to return to America or to return any further Bruce property. Still investing in stocks, he lost the money he had taken from Sasha. He got away with theft. Did he also get away with murder? Many people in Virginia think so.

CHAPTER 13

THE PARKWAY KILLER—OR KILLERS

The scenic Colonial Parkway cuts a great *S* through Tidewater Virginia, beginning at Jamestown, going beneath Colonial Williamsburg by means of a tunnel, and, after skirting the York River, ends at Yorktown. It's a lovely, peaceful drive, popular with college students, tourists, and picnicking families.

Or it was until the night of October 11, 1986, when two young women were savagely murdered there.

The two, Rebecca Ann Dowski, a twenty-one-year-old student, and Kathleen Marian Thomas, a twenty-seven-year-old stockbroker in Norfolk, Virginia, set out on the warm autumn evening, following the curving, tree-lined road to a pull-off popular with gay and lesbian couples.

A jogger out for a run the next morning noticed a Honda Civic down an embankment on the parkway, half hidden by shrubbery, about seven miles from Williamsburg. The bodies of Dowski and Thomas were found in the backseat of the car. The two women had last been seen at a party in Williamsburg.

Their purses were found in the car, intact, which ruled out robbery.

Both women were fully clothed, and there was no evidence of sexual assault. Their throats and wrists had signs of rope burns, indicating they had been bound, and both had been strangled and their throats slit by a very sharp instrument. Their bodies had then been doused with a flammable liquid, and matches were found in the car, leading police to believe that the murderer tried to burn the vehicle and destroy evidence of the women's identity. Police theorized that the killer, failing in the attempt to set the vehicle and the victims on fire, then tried to push the car into the York River.

Rebecca Ann Dowski, from Poughkeepsie, New York, was a student at the nearby College of William and Mary in Williamsburg, majoring in business management. Kathleen Thomas, from Lowell, Massachusetts, was one of the first women to graduate from the U.S. Naval Academy at Annapolis.

Both were healthy and athletic. Dowski had played sports at William and Mary, and Thomas had been trained in self-defense at the Naval Academy. How had they been overcome by their killer? And why? Were they stalked? Were they the killer's intended victims for some personal reason? Or were the killings random?

An early theory in the investigation was that they might have been killed by a rogue CIA commando in training at nearby Camp Peary. Also near the parkway are Yorktown Naval Weapons Station and the former DuPont explosives factory, now known as Cheatham Annex. Did someone who knew Thomas at the Naval Academy have a reason to kill her and her lover?

At the time, no one knew that these questions would be asked over and over in the next few years. This was not an isolated killing, but the first of at least four such murders, always of a couple in a vehicle.

Nearly a year passed before the next two victims were murdered. This murder occurred at Ragged Island Wildlife Refuge, on the south side of the James River, a popular hangout for homosexuals. But the victims were not gay, so at first the connection was not made with the Dowski-Thomas murders. David Knobling, twenty years old, and Robin Edwards, only fourteen, had met at an arcade on the afternoon of September 19, 1987, and they, along with Knobling's brothers, had cruised around in David's pickup. The young men had then taken Edwards home. The brothers went to the Knobling home, but David left again soon afterward and didn't return that night.

On Monday morning Knobling's pickup was discovered at the edge of the wildlife refuge with the keys in the ignition, the engine running. The driver's side door was open, and the window was half down. It had been raining the night before, so it was very unusual for the vehicle to have been left open to the elements. The truck's radio was on, and Knobling's wallet lay on the dashboard. The two occupants had obviously left the vehicle in a hurry, even leaving behind underwear and a pair of sneakers. Authorities suspected the worst for Edwards and Knobling.

Edwards's parents thought she had run away, and that morning they were waiting for the Social Services office to open so that they could report their daughter missing when police contacted them. Knobling was a legal adult and kept his own hours, so his parents didn't suspect tragedy until the pickup truck was found unoccupied. They suspected the worst but held out some hope that Robin and David would be found alive.

Two days later the bodies washed ashore about two miles down the river from Ragged Island. Knobling was wearing jeans. Edwards had on jeans with the belt unfastened and a white blouse. Her bra was pushed up around her neck. Police theorized that the two were forced from the pickup and made to walk ahead of their killer or killers through the refuge to an abandoned pier. There they were shot in the back of the head and dumped into the James River.

At this point there was little to connect the two cases, for the killings were so different. The murders had occurred on opposite sides of the James. In the first murders, both women were fully clothed and not assaulted. Edwards and Knobling were partially clothed, and there was some reason to believe that Edwards had been sexually assaulted. The two women were strangled, had their throats cut, and were doused in flammable material. Edwards and Knobling were shot. The main similarities were being in a vehicle as a couple and being in a park. Were the killings even related? Had the killer come to Ragged Island seeking a homosexual couple to kill and stumbled on Robin

Edwards and David Knobling? Was it random, or had the killer experimented with a new way of killing, a new kind of victim?

One obvious conclusion was that the killer very likely wore a uniform of some kind, approached the vehicles with a badge and flashlight, and asked for ID. Both murdered drivers were law-abiding and would have reached for their purse or wallet, perhaps expecting a ticket or at least a warning for parking beside a public road. Then the killer or killers must have brought out a weapon. At this point, it was too late for the victims to escape.

Numerous tips poured in to the police on both sides of the James and to the U.S. Park Service, which administers the Colonial Parkway, but all the leads proved to be dead ends.

Another eight months passed.

On April 8, 1988, Cassandra Lee Hailey and Richard Keith Call, both students at Christopher Newport College in Newport News, went out on their first date—and their last. When neither had returned by morning, their parents reported them missing.

Call's brother drove along the Colonial Parkway about 4:30 a.m. the following morning and saw a car that resembled Keith's with the driver's side door open and the trunk open. Another driver, on his way to work at 5:30 a.m., also saw the car with the driver's side door open. At 9:00 a.m. a park ranger found the red Toyota Celica on the parkway. Call's watch lay on the dashboard, Hailey's purse on the backseat. Their clothing was also on the backseat.

An early theory was that Call and Hailey had disrobed and gone for a swim in the York River, but water temperature in the river in early April would have been forty degrees or below. They would have tested the water and then raced back to the warmth of their car.

Despite extensive searching, no trace was ever found of the couple, and they are presumed dead.

A second set of murders had now occurred on the Colonial Parkway, which led newscasters to refer to the assailant as "the parkway killer." There was no denying that the authorities were dealing with a serial killer.

Again the modus operandi had changed: from fully clothed, to partially clothed, to totally undressed victims; and from leaving bodies where they would be found, to disposing of them in the river where they might be found, to taking away the bodies to some isolated spot where they would never be discovered.

The common element was the half-opened car, suggesting that one or more uniformed persons had approached the vehicle.

Construction of the Colonial Parkway, site of two of the murders, was begun in 1930 and completed in time for the visit in 1957 of Queen Elizabeth and Prince Philip to Virginia on the 350th anniversary of the Jamestown settlement. It was always intended to be noncommercial, sheltered by trees from nearby interstate traffic. The overpasses and bridges are faced with red brick so that the parkway looks "colonial." Wildlife is often sighted along its twenty-seven-mile length.

Joggers, hikers, and motorists now hesitated to use this beautiful road. Would there be another murder on the parkway?

The next murder occurred not on the secluded Colonial Parkway, but at a rest stop along busy Interstate 64 in New Kent County, a few miles north of Williamsburg. Annemarie Phelps, eighteen years old, from Virginia Beach, was engaged to Clifton Lauer of Amelia County. Phelps and her fiancé's brother, twenty-one-year-old Daniel Lauer, were driving in Lauer's car from Phelps's house on their way to Amelia when they disappeared. Witnesses reported seeing them the afternoon of September 5, 1989, between noon and 1:00 p.m. at the westbound rest stop on I-64. When they failed to arrive at Lauer's home, their families reported them missing. The car was located and identified at 5:30 p.m., only a short time after their disappearance. The car had nearly a full tank of gasoline, the keys were in the ignition, and Phelps's purse was in the car along with some of Lauer's clothing.

Despite a search, the couple could not be found. How could they have been taken in broad daylight from a public area?

A month later hunters found the two bodies in the woods about a mile from the rest stop, covered with a blanket and fallen leaves. Because of hot weather during September, the bodies were so decomposed that it was impossible to determine how Lauer had died. Phelps had been stabbed.

The details of the four gruesome killings went out to radio and television stations and newspapers all over America. Several women in Tidewater Virginia reported to police that they had been pursued by a man driving a car with a flashing light who attempted to pull them over, even though they had not been speeding or otherwise breaking the law. Being alone, they had refused to stop, and although their pursuer could clearly see their license number, there had never been a follow-up summons. Could these women have been the parkway killer's next intended victims?

Police warned drivers not to stop for uniformed men unless they were driving clearly marked law enforcement vehicles. In all other cases, drivers were instructed to drive to the next police station. If they had committed a traffic offense, they could be ticketed at the station.

Criminal profilers from the FBI office at Quantico, Virginia, collected details about the killings, attempting to profile the murderer or murderers. Since at least two couples had been killed on federal property, the murders were federal crimes.

Larry McCann, spokesman for the FBI, described the likely assailants. There were probably two men. The front man would approach the driver's side of the vehicle; the second man would be backup, ready with ropes, tape, and weapons, to help subdue the victims. The main killer likely was a white man, in his thirties or early forties, who wanted to be a policeman or a military commando, or who had recently been fired by a police department or had failed to be hired. He wanted to show the police how clever he was, that he could kill and get away with it.

THE DAILY PRESS-NEWPORT NEWS

A hiker walks along the Colonial Parkway between Williamsburg and Yorktown, site of savage, unsolved murders between 1986 and 1989.

The four sets of murders were featured on the television series *Unsolved Mysteries* and *Real Stories of the Highway Patrol* and were the subject of a book by Patricia Cornwell.

In 1988 the FBI questioned John Little, a New Zealand native, who claimed that there was a connection between Liberty Security Services and the murders. He also claimed to know who the next victims would be.

The mother of murder victim Robin Edwards had worked for Liberty Security. In April 1988, about the time of the Call-Hailey disappearances, the body of Laurie Ann Powell, who had worked as a receptionist for Liberty Security, was found floating near where the James and Elizabeth rivers converge. She had been murdered. Brian Craig Pettinger stopped working for Liberty Security in August 1988. The following February he was found in the James River, a drowning victim. A sinister connection, or just a coincidence? There was a connection, but to only one set of murders. What about the others?

For a while, the killings stopped.

Then in 1996 two young women were killed in Shenandoah National Park in western Virginia, in circumstances very much like those of the parkway killings.

Julianne Williams, twenty-four years old, of St. Cloud, Minnesota, and Laura ("Lollie") Winans, twenty-eight, of Unity, Maine, had met the previous summer when they both worked for Woodswomen, Inc., a Minnesota organization that, ironically, educates women in outdoor skills. The two became lovers and were planning to live together in Vermont, where Williams had a job. Winans had a month between the end of her school year and starting work in Vermont. The two decided to visit the park before packing and moving. Both were experienced hikers and backpackers and physically fit, and Williams had worked in another national park, Big Bend. They drove down to the park with Winans's golden retriever, Taj, signed in with the rangers at the northern park entrance, and got a camping permit for two nights. After camping and hiking for two days, they extended their camping permit for two more nights.

On May 24 they were tired out from hiking and accepted a ride from a ranger to the parking lot near Skyland Lodge. It was the last time they were seen alive. When Williams and Winans failed to return for appointments, alarms went out. Something was wrong.

On June 1 Winans's dog Taj was seen wandering near the lodge. Rangers searched the area and found the women's bodies at their campsite in a clearing only half a mile from the busy lodge. Their hands had been bound, their mouths taped, and their throats slashed so deeply they were almost decapitated. Winans was found inside the tent. Williams was found down the hill toward a stream, encased in her sleeping bag.

The National Park Service delayed announcing the murders for two days, allowing the killer and possible witnesses to leave. Only campers are required to have permits. Hundreds of cyclists, hikers, and motorists traveled through the park during those crucial days, which coincided with Memorial Day. Even when announcing the deaths, the Park Service called the slayings "an isolated incident." Others could have been murdered in the meantime.

The authorities estimated that the deaths took place sometime between May 27 and June 1. The last photos they took with their cameras were dated May 24, as were their last journal entries.

The following month the case was featured on the television show *America's Most Wanted*. Tips poured in, and the Park

Service estimates that they have followed up on fifteen thousand leads.

A suspect was arrested the following year, because of his attack on another woman. Darrell Dean Rice repeatedly drove his truck toward a young Canadian woman on a bicycle, finally knocking her off and pursuing her. She managed to get behind a tree as a ranger approached. Rice was arrested just before leaving the park, and he had already changed his shirt and replaced the missing plates on his truck. He spouted anti-women remarks, and he had been fired from his previous job for peculiar behavior toward women.

Could Rice have been the killer of Williams and Winans? He was videotaped entering Shenandoah National Park on May 25 and again on May 26, two of the days when the murders might have taken place.

Rice was arrested, jailed, and brought to trial, but DNA evidence on the duct tape placed over Williams's mouth indicated that someone else had bound her. There was nothing except Rice's presence in the park on two critical days and his attitude toward women to tie him to the killings, and charges against him were dropped.

Could the killer of Williams and Winans have also been the Colonial Parkway killer? It's possible. Interstate 64 goes from one site to the other, and the circumstances of the Shenandoah National Park killing and the first Colonial Parkway killing are eerily similar: two lesbian lovers in their twenties, alone together in federally owned property, unarmed, bound, with their throats slashed.

Why have the killings stopped? McCann, the FBI profiler, says there are several possible reasons: The killer's partner may have died, probably in some violent way, and the murderer might be uneasy about killing on his own. Or he may be in jail or may have moved away. If the killer has moved away, McCann says that he probably went to a Third World country. McCann searches the databases for similar murders in countries that keep and publish up-to-date records, but he has found no such indications. If the murderer is in jail, he may start killing again when he is released.

And there is another terrible possibility: The person who killed while impersonating a policeman may have finally been hired as a policeman or a security guard, which could give him a shield of protection for future killings.

Hikers, joggers, cyclists, and motorists still use the scenic highway, but they may think twice before pulling off to park at night.

CHAPTER 14

WHY THE SHORTS?

Mary, Michael, and Jennifer Short seemed the typical, loving family. In a portrait, the parents are close together, with a smiling nine-year-old Jennifer standing behind them, touching them both. The family lived modestly in a brick rancher in the village of Oak Level in Henry County, Virginia.

Why would anyone want to kill the Short family? And yet, someone did, in the early hours of August 15, 2002.

Henry County, southwest of Roanoke, had been going through economic hard times, with layoffs at the textile mills that once employed hundreds. Still, neighbors knew one another, and people were making do. It was high season for vegetable gardens, for picking berries, and for buying peaches at local orchards. There were lawns to mow, canning to be done, and school supplies to buy for the opening of the fall semester. Jennifer Short was excited about entering the fourth grade at Figsboro Elementary School.

It didn't seem a time for murder.

Michael Short owned and operated a mobile home moving business, and on the morning of August 15, one of his employees, Christopher Thompson, went to the Short home around 9:00 to drive Michael to Christiansburg to buy a new truck. He came upon a gruesome discovery: Michael lay dead in the carport, shot at close range. Thompson summoned Henry County sheriff's deputies, who entered the silent house and found Mary Short in her bed, also shot dead. The killings weren't random. The phone line to the house had been cut, and the murders took place between midnight and 9:00 a.m., when the victims would have been asleep. Both Mary and Michael had been shot at close range with a .22-caliber gun, a type difficult to trace from the spent shell casings. The murders were not a robbery gone wrong, as Michael's wallet was in his pocket, with $70 in it, and nothing of monetary value was missing from the house.

Jennifer was nowhere to be found. Her bed had been slept in, and the sheets were pulled back, but there was no sign of a struggle. Had she heard the shots and slid out of bed to go investigate? Or had she witnessed the murder of her mother and fled in fear for her life?

The deputies threw yellow crime scene tape around the house and began to search for Jennifer. Over the next few days, they searched the woods and a pond near the house and looked inside abandoned cars. Search dogs picked up Jennifer's scent in the wooded area and at the convenience store and motel close to the Short home, but she was known to have gone to those places in the days before her disappearance. Deputies even searched an area beside the highway because a strange man was seen parked in the wrong direction, leaning over the rail and tossing something away. It may have been just a cigarette, but the authorities had to follow up any tips and leads that came in, no matter how vague they might seem. Helicopters flew over the scene, looking for anything unusual; an abandoned cabin was searched; and divers plumbed the waters of Philpott Reservoir. No trace of Jennifer was found.

Pictures of the Short family and word of the murders went out over all the news services, and pictures of Jennifer were posted in gas stations, restaurants, and shopping malls all over Virginia and North Carolina, including the convenience store where she had bought candy the day before her disappearance. An Amber Alert was issued for her. One family member, a retired pilot, used his influence to have her picture posted as far away as Mexico. The story of the murders was featured on the television series *America's Most Wanted* and *Inside Edition*.

As part of the investigation, police removed guns, ammunition, bedclothes, and personal items from the Short home. A second search warrant allowed them to take a cell phone, tax records, videotapes, an answering machine with an obscene message, clothing, and "items of a sexual nature." Sheriff Frank Cassell said of the latter removal, "Anytime you have a child abducted, you've got to assume it may have something to do with a sexual nature."

The police had a number of suspects, but none that panned out. One of the first to be questioned was Thompson, the man who had found Michael Short's body. He was also the last to see the Shorts alive, as he had been at the house until nearly midnight, helping Michael repair a truck. He had spent the night at the motel within sight of the Shorts' home. He had the opportunity, but no motive, and was soon eliminated as a suspect.

Next to be questioned were Michael's adult sons from earlier marriages, and they too were crossed off the list of possible killers.

Sheriff Cassell and his deputies questioned everyone who knew the Shorts: family members, Jennifer's teachers and classmates, church members, and people who had worked with Michael at M.S. Mobile Home Movers. It was difficult to locate many of the men Michael hired, as he had often employed migrants as temporary help in moving mobile homes. He paid these workers with cash for a few hours' work, so there was no record of their names and addresses.

At the time of his murder, Michael Short was attempting to get a job with a mobile home moving company in coastal South Carolina. Police attempted to track down anyone he had talked to about the job, as well as the suppliers, contractors, and customers with whom he had dealt in 2001 and 2002. Moreover, the Shorts' house had been listed for sale, and in the days before the murders numerous potential buyers had walked through the house and would have known the location of bedrooms, phone lines, and other significant details.

The Henry County sheriff's department followed up more than three thousand leads; interviewed hundreds of people, some of them more than once; and administered numerous polygraph tests. The department soon ran out of money to pay the deputies for overtime work on the case. The sheriff asked for and got financial help from the state to continue with the investigation of the hideous crime that frightened people all over the area.

Calls came in from various people who thought they had spotted Jennifer. Police in Danville, mistakenly thinking they had found the missing nine-year-old, kept a sobbing girl in a police cruiser until her distraught parents produced ample identification. Two calls came from Winston-Salem, North Carolina. A man reported that he had seen a girl who looked like Jennifer in a blue truck, riding with a gray-haired man in his late thirties who had a beard and mustache. The truck driver, who was stopped at a light, pointed a handgun at the informant, who fled. The second call came from a woman who said she had seen a girl resembling Jennifer at a convenience store with a brown-haired man who had a beard and mustache. The sighting was near the previous caller's location. This man also was reported to have a gun. However, this time he drove an older white car. Could these two informants have seen the same man, who, realizing he had been spotted, had stolen a white car? The descriptions of the man and his possession of a handgun were eerily similar. Neither informant had managed to get a license number, and the sightings could not be confirmed.

Nearly five hundred people wearing yellow ribbons attended a wake for Michael and Mary Short at the Martinsville Church of God, and the couple were buried on August 23.

On September 2, the Henry County sheriff's office had Michael's body exhumed to take hair samples. Rumors spread that new evidence had emerged and that the hair samples were crucial. The truth was simpler: No samples had been taken at the autopsy.

A rumor soon spread that tests would determine that Michael was not Jennifer's biological father. The sheriff's department did nothing to stop the rumor. It was only later, after Jennifer had been found, that Sheriff Cassell stated that Michael was indeed Jennifer's father and that the department had known the truth all along. He had let the rumor fester in case the kidnapper was fantasizing that he was Jennifer's father. In that case, he might treat her better and keep her alive longer.

There were two "persons of interest" that the sheriff was unable to locate or identify. One was a white male seen driving a white single-cab truck near the Shorts' home the morning the bodies were discovered. The other was a man who had harassed Mary Short in 1992 when she worked at Pluma Textile Company. Authorities had removed him from the premises, but he continued to return, in effect stalking Mary. Could he have carried a grudge for ten years and finally acted on his anger? Had he been the person who made the obscene call?

Michael Short's uncle went on television asking the kidnapper to return Jennifer to a Walmart or any public place and to leave her with a note giving her name and the Henry County sheriff's telephone number. This, like many other pleas, went unanswered. Meanwhile, Mary Short's sister and brother-in-law filed for custody of Jennifer when she was found.

Leads on the case dwindled even as a reward for the return of Jennifer and a solution to her parents' murders rose to $67,000. Psychics called the sheriff's office, offering to help find the missing girl, but none had any useful information.

The FBI released this sketch of a "person of interest" seen in a white truck near the Shorts' home the morning of their murders.

FBI WEB SITE

Word came from West Virginia that the skeletal remains of a child had been found in Greenbrier Forest State Park; however, tests showed that they did not belong to Jennifer. Someone else's missing child was now confirmed dead.

Then, in late September, a call came from the Rockingham County, North Carolina, sheriff, Sam Page. He thought Jennifer's remains might have been found, at a site that was about thirty miles south of where Jennifer had lived. A man in Stoneville had been out walking with his dog when the dog brought him what he thought was a discarded brown wig. When he touched the hair, he discovered to his horror that it was attached to a skull. Combing the area underneath a bridge where the skull was discovered, Sheriff Page and his deputies found rib bones. Further searches turned up no more remains. The deputies checked a nearby cemetery to make certain that no graves had been disturbed and their bones scattered.

Cassell at first doubted that the remains were Jennifer's. The hair color didn't look quite right. Still, he took possession of the remains and sent them to the Virginia crime lab in Roanoke. DNA testing showed that this was indeed Jennifer. She had been shot once in the head. There was no way to determine how long she had lived after being kidnapped or how she had been snatched away from her home without a struggle.

A funeral was held on October 9, with Sheriff Cassell and his deputies serving as pallbearers. Photos and videos of the smiling, brown-haired child were shown—Jennifer in happier times, playing softball, celebrating birthdays. Jennifer was buried next to her parents. The mystery of her whereabouts had been solved, and her grieving relatives had some sort of closure—at least they knew that she was not being abused or tortured. But her killer was out there somewhere, and family and friends as well as the authorities were determined to find him and bring him to justice. The sheriff's department had been joined in the effort by the Virginia state police; the Rockingham County, North Carolina, sheriff's office; and the FBI.

Another call came from North Carolina, this one fingering a suspect. Gary Lemons, who rented to a retired carpenter, Gary Bowman, reported strange behavior by his tenant that seemed to tie him to the Short case. Bowman, he said, had a map in his mobile home with a circle around Henry County, and he had threatened to kill a mobile home mover in Virginia who had not followed through on an agreement to move his mobile home. He also said that Bowman was building a false bottom in his van. Moreover, Bowman packed up and moved to Canada the day after Mary and Michael Short's bodies were found. Bowman's home was only a mile from where Jennifer's remains were found underneath a bridge.

Rockingham County deputies searched Bowman's home and took away bedding, cushions, hair samples, a vacuum cleaner, and phone records.

Canadian authorities deported Bowman. He was brought to Henry County and questioned extensively. There was no physical evidence to connect Gary Bowman to the murders and abductions, so he was released on October 30, 2002. Over the next few years, the shadow of suspicion continued to hang over him, and he was shunned. Finally, in 2007, the FBI announced that Bowman was no longer a suspect.

In December 2002 Michael Fulcher, a prisoner in Bland Correctional Facility and a frequent informant for the police, offered to share information about the Short murders in return for a shorter sentence. He was serving time for money laundering,

167

drug running, and firearms charges. After talking privately with him, investigators found his information too vague to be of any help. The presiding judge indicated that he would be open to a lesser sentence if Fulcher had more information, but no more was offered.

By the first anniversary of the murders, the police had not yet arrested a suspect. Authorities in Rockingham County had diverted the stream where Jennifer's remains were found but had not discovered any new clues. Some critics thought it should have been done immediately after the skull was found. Anyone could have gone to the site in the meantime and removed incriminating evidence.

The investigation dragged on, with few concrete results. It was sidetracked in November 2006 when Sheriff Cassell and twelve of his employees, as well as a postal employee, a probation officer, and five civilians, were arrested on charges of stealing and selling guns and drugs that had been seized as evidence. Sheriff Cassell was charged with lying to federal authorities to protect his department. The former state trooper, who had been first elected sheriff in 1991 and reelected several times since, was found guilty and served eight months in a federal prison in Pennsylvania.

This meant that the remaining deputies and the new sheriff, Lane Perry, were short-handed. Investigators who might have worked on the Short case had to put it aside and handle current murders and other crimes. Efforts to find the Shorts' killer or killers were at a standstill.

More than five years after the murders, the FBI set up a special task force devoted to the case. In addition to placing prominent photos of the murdered family on the FBI Web site, detectives released an age-enhanced sketch of a man seen outside the Shorts' home the morning of the murders. He was thought to be in his forties, with the weathered complexion one might expect from an outdoor worker. He was driving a white single-cab two-ton flatbed truck, described by a witness as being a 1998–2002 model, similar to an International.

Each year on the anniversary of the murders, a procession of motorcycle riders, cyclists, and hikers makes its way from the brick rancher where the Shorts lived to the bridge in Stoneville, North Carolina, where Jennifer's remains were found. A wreath is placed on the bridge in her memory, and funds are raised to keep the reward active for whoever comes forward with information on her killer.

Henry County deputy Curtis Spence, who has worked on the case from the beginning, still has a photo of Jennifer Short taped in his vehicle where he can see it as he goes about his duty. Someday, he hopes, the man who gunned down a couple in their home and robbed an innocent child of her life will be found and convicted.

BIBLIOGRAPHY

BOOKS AND PERIODICALS

"A Block of Fine Marble," *Virginia Cavalcade*, Winter 1955.

Alexander, Ann Field. *Race Man: The Rise and Fall of the "Fighting Editor," John Mitchell*. Charlottesville, Virginia: University of Virginia Press, 2002.

Alexandra Bruce Michaelides' obituary, *The Danville Register*, November 12, 1975.

Allen, Mike. "Aunt, Uncle File for Custody of Girl as Search Continues," *The Roanoke Times*, September 20, 2002.

———. "FBI Seeks Leads on Truck Seen Near Shorts' House," *The Roanoke Times*, January 17, 2009.

———. "Mystery of Who Killed the Shorts Remains Unsolved 1 Year After," *The Roanoke Times*, August 15, 2003.

———. "Nonstop Search for Jennifer Short, 9, Takes Its Toll," *The Roanoke Times*, September 8, 2002.

An Inventory of the Contents of the Governor's Palace Taken after the Death of Lord Botetourt. Williamsburg, Virginia: Colonial Williamsburg Foundation, 1981.

"Argument Now On: Jury Will Decide Fate of Mrs. Victor Hall Today," *The Daily News Record*, Harrisonburg, Virginia, August 8, 1914, p. 6.

Ayers, Edward L. *Vengeance and Justice: Crime and Punishment in the 19th Century American South*. New York: Oxford University Press, 1984.

Beevor, Antony, and Artemis Cooper. "Obituary: Evangeline Bruce," *The London Independent*, December 15, 1995.

Bigelow, Alden D. "Mystery in the Crypt: Was Governor Botetourt Buried at William and Mary College?" *Virginia Cavalcade*, Spring 1984.

Blackburn, Joyce. *George Wythe of Virginia*. New York: Harper & Row, 1973.

"Bookmarked: A Gift from Above," *The University of Virginia Magazine*, Spring 2009.

Boyd, Julian P., and W. Edwin Hemphill. *The Murder of George Wythe*. Williamsburg, Virginia: Institute of Early American History and Culture, 1955.

Brandau, J. K. *Murder at Green Springs*. New York: Morgan-James Publishing, 2007.

Brown, Imogene E. *American Aristides: A Biography of George Wythe*. East Brunswick, New Jersey: Associated University Presses, 1981.

Burr, George Lincoln, ed. *Narratives of the Witchcraft Cases.* New York: Charles Scribner's Sons, 1914.

Campbell, Beverly, "When Virginia Ducked Milady Witch," *Richmond Times-Dispatch,* December 30, 1934.

Chadwick, Bruce, *I Am Murdered.* New York: John Wiley & Sons, 2009.

Crean, Ellen, "Townspeople mourn Jennifer Short," *Martinsville Bulletin,* October 12, 2002.

Dabney, Virginius. *Mr. Jefferson's University.* Charlottesville: University Press of Virginia, 1981.

———. *Richmond: The Story of a City.* Charlottesville: University Press of Virginia, 1990.

———. *Virginia: The New Dominion.* New York: Doubleday, 1971.

"Defense in the Trial of Mrs. Victor Hall Closed Its Case," *The Daily News Record,* Harrisonburg, Virginia, August 6, 1914, p. 6.

"Expect Verdict in Hall Case at Louisa Today," *The Daily News Record,* Harrisonburg, Virginia, August 7, 1914, p. 6.

"Failed to Show Motive," *The Daily News Record,* Harrisonburg, Virginia, August 11, 1914, p. 5.

"Former Norfolk Mayor Slain," *The Danville Bee,* March 4, 1972.

Genovese, Eugene D. *Roll, Jordan, Roll: The World the Slaves Made.* New York: Random House, 1972.

Hall, Debbie. "New Sketch Released in Short Investigation," *Martinsville Bulletin,* March 17, 2009.

———. "Short Case Still Haunts Sergeant," *Martinsville Bulletin,* August 14, 2009.

Hamilton, Charles Henry. *Peter Francisco, Soldier Extraordinary.* Richmond, Virginia: Whittet & Shepperson, 1976.

Huger, Thomas B. "Tom Mason at the Throttle," *Virginia Cavalcade,* Autumn 1984.

Innis, P. B., and Walter Dean. *Gold in the Blue Ridge.* Washington, DC: Robert B. Luce, 1973.

Jacoby, Susan. "Public Service and Private Pain," *The New York Times,* October 10, 1982.

Jameson, W. C. *Buried Treasures of the South.* Little Rock, Arkansas: August House Publishers, 1992.

"Judge Overrules Plea in Hall Conviction," *Petersburg Daily Progress,* August 14, 1914.

Kelley, Robin D. G., and Earl Lewis, eds. *To Make Our World Anew: A History of African Americans from 1880.* New York: Oxford University Press, 2000.

Kurth, Peter. *Anastasia: The Riddle of Anna Anderson.* Boston: Little, Brown, 1983.

Kyle, Louisa Venable. *The Witch of Pungo and Other Stories.* Virginia Beach: Four O'Clock Farms Publishing, 1973.

Lankford, Nelson D. *The Last American Aristocrat: The Biography of Ambassador David K. E. Bruce.* Boston: Little, Brown, 1996.

Lebsock, Suzanne. *A Murder in Virginia.* New York: W. W. Norton, 2003.

Massie, Robert. *The Romanovs: The Final Chapter.* New York, Random House, 1995.

McCaffery, Jen, and Mike Allen. "Man Offers a Tip on Short Case for Lesser Sentence," *The Roanoke Times*, December 10, 2002.

Mellin, Joan. *Privilege: The Enigma of Sasha Bruce.* New York: New American Library, 1982.

Mills, Charles A. *Treasure Legends of Virginia.* Alexandria, Virginia: Apple Cheeks Press, 1984.

"Mrs. Hall Released on Bail Pending Appeal," *The Daily News Record*, Harrisonburg, Virginia, August 15, 1914, p. 7.

"Mrs. Victor Hall Goes on the Stand as Last Witness in Own Behalf," *The Daily News Record*, Harrisonburg, Virginia, August 3, 1914, p. 6.

Nelson, Robert F. *Stirring Legends of Virginia in the American Revolution.* Richmond, Virginia: Whittet & Shepperson, 1974.

———. *Thrilling Legends of Virginia*. Richmond, Virginia: Whittet & Shepperson, 1971.

"The Papers of William Frederick Duckworth," Special Collection, Old Dominion University Library, Norfolk, Virginia.

"Peter Francisco Day," Legislative Moments in Virginia History, presented to the Virginia General Assembly by the Virginia Historical Society, February 24, 2004.

Power-Waters, Alma. *Virginia Giant: The Story of Peter Francisco*. New York: E. P. Dutton, 1957.

"The Press: Quest for a Personality," *Time*, September 5, 1960.

"Psychologist: Parkway Killer Probably Had Partner," *The Daily Press*, Newport News, Virginia, June 22, 1992.

Shapira, Ian. "After Toil and Trouble, 'Witch' Is Cleared," *The Washington Post*, July 12, 2006.

Swift, Earl. "The Duckworth File: A Lead amid Faded Hope," *The Virginian Pilot*, August 26, 2007.

———. "The Duckworth File: Case Falls into Obscurity," *The Virginian Pilot*, August 25, 2007.

———. "The Duckworth File: Casting for Leads," *The Virginian Pilot*, August 20, 2007.

———. "The Duckworth File: Cops Feel the Heat," *The Virginian Pilot*, August 21, 2007.

————. "The Duckworth File: Sifting the Victim's Past," *The Virginian Pilot*, August 22, 2007.

————. "The Duckworth File: Theories and Walls," *The Virginian Pilot*, August 24, 2007.

————. "The Duckworth File: Who Shot a Former Norfolk Mayor?" *The Virginian Pilot*, August 19, 2007.

————. "The Duckworth File: Years of Enemies," *The Virginian Pilot*, August 23, 2007.

Tarter, Brent. "Lord Botetourt's Warming Machine," *Virginia Cavalcade*, Winter 1980.

"Virginia Woman Seeks to Clear Witch of Pungo," *USA Today*, July 9, 2006.

Weiss, Eric. "Alert on Girl Yields Calls But No Clues," *The Washington Post*, August 19, 2002.

Williams, Reed. "Police Lack Suspects in Short Slayings," *The Roanoke Times*, August 12, 2007.

"The Witchcraft Delusion Rejected," *Virginia Cavalcade*, Summer 1956.

NEWS BROADCASTS AND WEB SITES

Absoluteastronomy.com/topics/Seven_Society, May 7, 2009.

Cable News Network, "Jailed Man Questioned in Jennifer Short Murder," October 8, 2002.

Emery, Marcus. "Who Killed Norfolk's Mayor Duckworth?" Helium.com, August 7, 2009.

Federal Bureau of Investigation Web site, www.fbi.gov/wanted/seek_info/Short_murders, January 2009.

FoxNews.com, "Jennifer Short's Remains Identified," October 4, 2002.

FoxNews.com, "Police: Suspect May Be Someone Known to Short Family," August 17, 2002.

FoxNews.com, "Two Say They Saw Jennifer Short, Armed Man in Same Area," August 21, 2002.

Freewarehof.org/manahans, August 13, 2009.

historynet.com/the-mysterious-death-of-judge-george-wythe.htm, May 26, 2009.

historynet.com/peter-francisco-remarkable-american-revolutionary-war-soldier, July 5, 2009.

journalismclass.wmblogs.net/2009/05/19/the-colonial-parkway-murders.

labyrinth13.com/mirror/VirginiaMurders/index, July 23, 2009.

orderwhitemoon.org/goddess/GSherwood, May 6, 2009.

parkway.crimeshadows.com/main, July 23, 2009.

spiritus-temporis.com/seven_society, May 7, 2009.

virginiabeachhistory.org/kyle, May 4, 2009.

Wikipedia.org/wiki/Bunny_Man, April 20, 2009.

Wikipedia.org/wiki/Charles_Thompson_(admiral), July 13, 2009.

Wikipedia.org/wiki/Colonial_Parkway_Killer, April 20, 2009.

Wikipedia.org/wiki/Norwegian_Lady_Statues, April 20, 2009.

Wikipedia.org/wiki/Norborne_Berkeley,_4th_Baron_ Botetourt, May 6, 2009.

Wikipedia.org/wiki/Seven_Society, April 20, 2009.

Wxii12.com/News/1627287, "Investigators Narrow Focus for Suspects." Posted August 22, 2002. Accessed August 28, 2009.

INDEX

Abernathy, Mary, 70, 71, 72–73, 74, 75, 78, 79, 80, 81

Anderson, Anna (and Anastasia). *See* Manahan Anderson, Anna

Barnes, Elizabeth, 5–6

Barnes, Mary, 70, 72–73, 75, 78, 81

Barnes, Pokey, 70, 71, 72–73, 74, 75, 78, 79–80, 81

Beale, Thomas Jefferson, 56–57, 57–59, 59–61, 65–66

Beale Treasure, 56–68

Beale Treasure code, 58, 59, 60, 61, 62–63, 63–65, 66–67

Berkeley, Norborne. *See* Botetourt, Baron

Boston, Channing, 87–88

Botetourt, Baron, 29–42

Botkin, Gleb, 112, 113–14

Bowman, Gary, 167

Broadnax, Lydia, 48, 49–50, 52, 54

Brown, Michael, 48, 49–50, 51, 52, 53

Bruce, David K. E.
  Ailsa Mellon (wife) and, 136
  children of, 136
  daughters' deaths, 134–35. *See also* Michaelides, Alexandra "Sasha" Bruce
  diplomatic positions of, 137
  Evangeline (wife) and, 136, 137, 140
  family history and prestige, 135
  legal career, 135
  wealth of, 136

Byrd, Anne, 3

Call, Richard Keith, 150–51

Cartwright, Alice, 3

Church Hill Tunnel, 102–5

Colonial Parkway murders. *See* parkway killer(s)

Creedle, Willie, 132

The Displaying of Supposed Witchcraft (Webster), 3

Dowski, Rebecca Ann, 146–48

Duckworth, Fred
  accomplishments and accolades, 127–28
  biographical sketch, 128–29
  citizens angered by, 121–22, 129–30
  closing schools for racial reasons, 122
  General Douglas MacArthur and, 121
  urban renewal of Norfolk and, 120–21, 129
  Virginia Beach and, 130

Duckworth, Fred, murder of
  autopsy results, 124–25
  confessed killer and, 131
  discovery of body, 122–23
  events leading to, 122
  funeral after, 128, 129
  gun used, 126–27
  investigation, 125–27
  Johnnie Ozlin and, 132
  professional hit theory, 124, 131
  reward for information about, 128, 130
  Ruth Hodges and, 122, 126, 131
  scene of, 122–24
  son-in-law, daughter and, 130, 132
  unconfirmed solution to, 132
  Willie Creedle and, 132

Dunkum, Asa "Acey," 88–89, 90

Dunkum, William Richard "Buck"
  arson perpetrated against, 91, 92

buying Hall's Store, 88–89
Dunkum's Store and, 91, 92, 96
losing store to fire, 92
running store after Acey's
   death, 90
selling interest in Hall's Store, 91
Victor Hall murder and, 93, 95, 96

Edwards, Robin, 148–50, 154

The False Anastasia (Gilliard), 110–11
Farrand, Phillip, 130, 132
Foushee, Dr. William, 50, 53, 55
Francisco, Peter (Pedro), 14–28
Fulcher, Michael, 167–68

Gayle, Ellen, 72–73
gentle giant. *See* Francisco, Peter
   (Pedro)
Gisburne family, 5–6
Grady, Katherine, 2
Greene, General Nathanael, 22–23
Gregory, Cass, 77, 80, 81

Hailey, Cassandra Lee, 150–51
Hall, Elizabeth Dunkum "Lizzie"
   Acey Dunkum and, 89, 90
   Bill Roberts and, 97
   boarders and servant of, 91–92
   conviction for Victor's murder,
      98–100
   depot/pantry fires and, 96–97
   doubt about murder conviction,
      99–100
   hiring detective to investigate
      Victor's murder, 95
   later years and death, 101
   marrying Victor, 90
   pardoned, 100–101
   photograph, 99
   prison sentence, 100
   rumors about Victor and, 90, 97
   suspicion/arrest for Victor's
      murder, 97–98
   witnessing Poindexter murder, 89

Hall, Victor
   autopsy of, 94
   investigation into murder of,
      94–95
   marrying Lizzie, 90
   murder of, 92–94
   parents and aunt living with,
      91–92
   photograph, 99
   rumors about Lizzie and, 90, 97
   as store clerk, 89
   as telegraph operator and depot
      manager, 90
Hall's Store, 87–101
   arson in and around, 91, 92,
      96–97
   broom factory and, 87, 88, 90, 91
   Channing Boston and, 87–88
   location and advantages of, 87
   Poindexter murder by, 89
   Roy McKnighton and, 88
   smallpox outbreak and, 88
   Yancey brothers and, 88
   See also Hall, Elizabeth Dunkum
      "Lizzie"; Hall, Victor
Halsey, Admiral William, 86
Harding, William, 3
Hart, Clayton, 64–65
Hazelwood, N. H., 63–64
Henry, Patrick, 16
Hodges, Ruth, 122, 126, 131
Hot Feet (IMP Society), 82–83
Houston, Sam, 21

IMP Society (Hot Feet), 82–83

Jefferson, Thomas
   Banastre Tarleton and, 23
   George Wythe and, 46, 47, 48
   on Lord Botetourt's death, 34
   statue of, Secret Seven Society and,
      85, 86
   writing Virginia constitution, 47
Jenkins, Jane, 3
Jennings, Annie, 112, 113

Kennedy, Senator Robert, 85
Knobling, David, 148–50

Lafayette, General, 18, 24, 26
Lauer, Daniel, 152

Manahan, John (Jack), 114–15, 117
Manahan Anderson, Anna
  Alexander Tchaikovsky and, 108–9
  Anastasia film and, 113
  Annie Jennings and, 112, 113
  British royal family position
    on, 118
  claiming to be Anastasia, 108–9
  death of, 115
  deformed foot of Anastasia
    and, 110
  The False Anastasia and, 110–11
  fate of Anastasia's family and,
    106–8, 116–17
  filing claims against Bank of
    England, 112–13
  forensic evidence about, 117,
    118–19
  marriage to Dr. John
    Manahan, 114
  in mental institution, 114
  in New York, 111–13
  paranoia of, 114–15
  photograph of John and, 117
  purported rape, pregnancy and
    marriage, 108–9
  Romanov fortune and, 112–
    13, 115
  Russian nobility opinions of, 109,
    110–12
  scientific links to Anastasia, 113
  Sergei Rachmaninoff and, 112
  story of escape from Russia, 108–9
  supporter Gleb Botkin and, 112,
    113–14
  tissue samples of, 115, 118
  World War II and, 113
Marable, Solomon, 71–72, 73–75,
  76–77, 78, 79, 80

Mason, Tom, 103
Mayo, Colonel William, 20
McCaw, Dr. James, 50, 53, 55
McClurg, Dr. James, 50, 53–54, 55
McConnell, James Rogers, 85
McKnighton, Roy, 88
Mellon, Ailsa, 136
Michaelides, Alexandra "Sasha" Bruce
  allure of Staunton Hill, 136, 140
  birth and siblings, 136
  boarding school education of, 137
  burial of, 143
  challenge of married men for, 137
  college, sex, drugs and, 138
  death haunting, 138
  Greek lover and gallery
    shenanigans, 139–40
  implausibility of suicide, 134
  Marios and. *See* Michaelides,
    Marios
  suicide issues of, 138, 139
  suspicious death of, 133–35, 143
  "what if" points of, 138
Michaelides, Marios
  abusing Sasha, 134, 141–42, 143
  charges/suit against, 144–45
  demanding estate settlement, 143
  first meeting Sasha, 140
  keeping marriage secret form Sasha,
    140–41
  marriage to Sasha, 142
  returning to Greece, 144
  reuniting with Mary (wife),
    143–44
  Sasha's death and, 133–35, 144–45
  stealing from Sasha, 141–42,
    143–44, 145
Morriss, Robert
  Beale investigating, 58
  death of, 62
  divulging treasure information,
    61–62
  entrusted with treasure
    information, 59–61
  integrity of, 58, 66

Nash, Belinda, 13
Nelson, William, 35
Nicholas, Philip Norborne, 52, 53
Nicholas, Robert Carter, 35, 36–37

Ozlin, Johnnie, 132

Page, Bobby, 84–85
parkway killer(s), 146–58
Peter Francisco Day, 23. *See also*
    Francisco, Peter (Pedro)
Pettinger, Brian Craig, 155
Phelps, Annemarie, 152
Poindexter family, 89
Pollard, Edward
    alibi of, 70
    David Thompson and, 77, 79
    discrepancy in time of Lucy's
        murder and, 71
    testimony of, 74, 79
Pollard, Lucy, murder of, 69–81
    arrest of suspects, 71–72
    brutality of, 71
    Cass Gregory and, 77, 80, 81
    change of venue for trials, 78–79
    confessions about, 73, 74–75, 76
    David Thompson and, 76, 77, 79,
        80, 81
    Ellen Gayle and, 72–73
    false accusations in, 73
    Mary Abernathy and, 70, 71,
        72–73, 74, 75, 78, 79, 80, 81
    Mary Barnes and, 70, 72–73, 75,
        78, 81
    Pokey Barnes and, 70, 71, 72–73,
        74, 75, 78, 79–80, 81
    problematic evidence in, 76
    publicity of, 73, 76, 78
    purported dispute leading to,
        77, 79
    Solomon Marable and, 71–72,
        73–75, 76–77, 78, 79, 80
    stolen money, valuables and, 70
    trials, appeals, and retrials for,
        73–75, 76–77, 78–80

unresolved questions about, 81
"winking man" at trial of, 75, 76
Poole, William W., 104
Powell, Laurie Ann, 154–55
Pungo, Witch of. *See Sherwood, Grace*
    references
Pungo Strawberry Festival, 13

Randolph, Edmund, 53, 55
Randolph, John, 35, 41
Rice, Darrell Dean, 157
Roberts, Bill, 97
Ross, T. W., 89

Secret Seven Society, 82–86
Sherwood, Grace, 1–13
Sherwood, Grace (Hill trial)
    accusations and beating, 6
    denying charges, 8–9
    formal charges, 7–8
    Hill assault verdict and, 6
    inspections for witchcraft evidence,
        6–7, 8
    posthumous pardon, 13
    sentence and resolution, 11
    Virginia prosecution guidelines
        and, 11–12
    water test and verdict, 9–11
    water test location, 12
    as Witch of Pungo, 12
Sherwood, James
    death of, 6
    defending charges against Grace,
        5–6
    marriage to Grace, 4
Short murders, 159–69
Somerset, Henry, 35–36
St. George, Hamilton, 46
Stettinius, Edward, 86
Sweeney, George Wythe
    arrest of, 51
    background of, 48
    evidence against, 50–52
    poisoning George Wythe and
        servants, 49–50

shady deeds of, 48–49
trial and acquittal of, 52–55

Tarleton, Banastre, 20, 23, 24
Tchaikovsky, Alexander, 108–9. *See also* Manahan Anderson, Anna
Thomas, Kathleen Marian, 146–48
Thompson, Charles, 30–31
Thompson, David, 76, 77, 79, 80, 81
Tunnel, Church Hill, 102–5

University of Virginia, Secret Seven Society, 82–86

vampire, in Church Hill Tunnel, 104–5

Ward, James, 62–63, 64–65, 66–67
White, John, 4
William and Mary College, 34, 41–42, 47, 48, 147
Williams, Julianne, 155–57
Winans, Laura "Lollie," 155–57
Winston, Judge Anthony, 15–16
Wirt, William, 52–53, 55
Wisner, Frank, 85–86
witchcraft
  Alice Cartwright and, 3
  Anne Byrd and, 3
  British statute against, 2
  fines for false accusations, 3
  Jane Jenkins and, 3
  Katherine Grady and, 2
  in Lower Norfolk County (Virginia Beach), 3
  "marks of the devil" and, 2
  tests for, 2
  through the ages, 1
  trials in colonial Virginia, 2–3
  Virginia prosecution guidelines, 11–12
  water "test," 2
  William Harding and, 3
  See also Sherwood, Grace references
Wythe, George, 43–55

attachment to Williamsburg, 45
Chesterville family estate and, 43–44, 45
claiming "I am murdered!," 43
Continental Congress and, 46–47
death and funeral, 52
deaths affecting, 43–44, 45, 48
designing Great Seal of Virginia, 47
doctors botching murder investigation of, 50–51, 53–54, 55
early years of, 43–44
education of, 44
George Wythe Sweeney and, 48–49, 50–54, 55
Governor Francis Fauquier and, 45–46
House of Burgesses and, 45
illustration of, 46
law practice of, 45
Lydia Broadnax and, 48, 49–50, 52, 54
marriages of, 45
Michael Brown and, 48, 49–50, 51, 52, 53
murderer's trial and acquittal, 52–55
passing bar, 44–45
poisoning of servants and, 48–55
reading law, 44
signing Declaration of Independence, 47
Thomas Jefferson and, 46, 47, 48
U.S. Constitution and, 47–48
as Virginia Court of Chancery chancellor, 48
at William and Mary College, 47, 48
writing Virginia constitution, 47

Yancey, Silas and Lewis, 88

Z Society, 83

ABOUT THE AUTHOR

Emilee Hines, a native Virginian, is fascinated with the history and people of her home state. She is a graduate of Lynchburg College and has a master's degree in history from the University of North Carolina in Chapel Hill. She has taught in Virginia and Kenya. This is her fourth book for Globe Pequot, and her first, *It Happened in Virginia*, is now in its second edition. Her other Globe Pequot titles are *More Than Petticoats: Remarkable Virginia Women* and the editorial portion of *Virginia: Mapping the Old Dominion State through History*. She was coauthor of the series *Old Virginia Houses* and is the author of a memoir, *East African Odyssey*, and *Burnt Station*, a novel, as well as 300 articles and short stories. She lives in the mountains of North Carolina. Her Web site is www.emileehines.com.